SHIPMATES

SHIPMATES

Before the Mast:
A Coastie's Chronicle of the Dishonorable

By Bradley Angle

Published by: Dirty Sailor Company

Pojack Shore / Bradley Angle
Visit the website at www.dirtysailorcompany.com
admin@dirtysailorcompany.com

Printed in the United States of America

First Printing: July 2019
Dirty Sailor Company

ISBN: 978-0-578-48989-6

Dedicated to all those who left the Coast Guard
under Other Than Honorable conditions.

Words from the Author

HELPING POJACK with his VA claim, and anticipated appeal, was my first and only intent. Then three things happened: 1) I read Dana's "Two Years Before the Mast," 2) the President made comments on a rereleased VA report, and 3) Captain Ladson Mills (Ret.) published "Abandoned Shipmates." The results build the pages of this book.

While reaching for his zipper, Pojack said: "It reeks of paradise 'neath this bridge—this bridge and every other mother-fucking bridge downtown—almost like lowtide."

I first stumbled upon him under interstate 480, where it spans the Missouri and connects Council Bluffs to Omaha. Covered in hairy rusted-red leather skin and faded tattoos, his vacant stare towards the flowing river didn't prevent me from asking him for a light. My question was not answered. He sat motionless, so I took the opportunity to stare myself. His ink was all nautical and old, Pacific crafted. The guy couldn't have been more than 40, but looked frail and weathered. Hair curled into a ball and tucked under a Coors Original ball cap. "How 'bout a light, there guy?" This time he turned. I first thought he was a crazy drunk by the way he said "huh?" The sound was raspy, like he'd been yelling his entire life, or his vocal muscles were coated with the contents of an ashtray. His eyes saw only where his head moved to direct them. First at my duct-taped sandals. Then slowly up to my shorts, stomach, beard, and finally my 7/11 shades. "I said, you got a match there fella? I'll get it right back to ya. Promise."

"I gotta lighter right here for ya." He smirked and reached for his crotch zipper.

That grin led to all of this... Within hours he relayed an experience so near to mine, I was dumbfounded at our fluke encounter. His stories captured identical characters that I'd met and lost along the way. Those of friends trapped in gutters and lost in dark convictions.

Encouraging Pojack to seek help through the VA seemed natural enough.

Richard Henry Dana Jr.'s "Two Years Before the Mast," was beside me and missing its cover by the end of that trip. Unlike Dana, and more like a sailor[1], I've been driven, in a flippant angst, to experience a world different than what the Officer Class prescribes as real or worthy. That drive is also in the text that follows, mixed with the inspiring thoughts that surfaced as I read "Two Years." Often, I wonder where all of my shipmates ventured to, marked by memories and scars, or pride-culture and medal-distinction. I'd wager the sea was lost on most; a nostalgia past represented with plastic keepsakes on the prow - Dick on the mantel.

Read the most recent (updated) report from the VA[2]: "VA National Suicide Data Report 2005–2016" (Affairs, 2018), and the most recent report from the CG, "State of Behavioral Health of the United States Coast Guard" (ICF International, 2013). It would be nice if the authors of these reports were fucked with two separate penises; one with gonasyphalitus, and the second one, a really big one, up the butt. There are biases, misleading and scandalous inferences, and mass generalizations in these documents, overwhelming so in the executive summaries. These research papers cannot be mapped onto the reality of our situation. We need to know the who's, what's and

---

[1] Sailor: A debatable term, though commonly used to describe a person who is engaged in the seagoing life style. The United States Naval Academy refuses to call officers "sailors," and refers only to enlisted men as such.

[2] VA: Department of Veterans Affairs

why's regarding veteran suffering, often leading to death or gutters. Specifically, we need data on behavioral health in the veteran group who does not use the VHA[3] (more than 50%), and we need info on those separated with "Other Than Honorable" conditions. These people are our shipmates... Why did the President demand the report from August 2016 be updated (to the report in question), with an even more incorrect and misleading summary?

As the first version of this text went through drafting, I was directed to a newly published book called "Abandoned Shipmates: The Destruction of Coast Guard Captain Ernie Blanchard," by Ladson Mills (Mills, 2019). Mills led me to a dissertation, titled "The Study of a Secret Society: Resistance to Open Discussion of Suicide in the United States Coast Guard" (Steinmetz, 2011). Both of these texts point to major problems in the US Coast Guard, all leading to unwarranted distress. Each of these texts influenced my decisions to spin my yarns to audiences outside of my nautical network. However, I wrote for myself, with love and loathing for the people I met and lost along the way. I am telling sea stories here, which may highlight some obvious issues, though this is no scholarly article.

My copyeditor Mike did not pick up on the italics throughout, which worries me. He also was concerned about the sailor lingo - "it will be difficult for non-sailors to read." And I agree, though the stories are from a sailor's head. As a compromise, I've inserted footnotes where I define the terms, including etymology where such a thing may be of value to *my own ego*. Thank you, Mike. Time is the strangest and most valuable asset we have, and you share yours often.

---

[3] VHA: Veterans Health Administration

If incest was not frowned upon, I would have regular sex with Brendon, J, David, and Dan. I'll take authentic over any other trait! We are all undoubtedly pushed and pulled by our surroundings, so it is nice to meet people who configure their surroundings to benefit their rare potential. Unique - the sign of an exceptional lifestyle...

In short, what started as one ex-Coastie trying to help another became something a bit more squally. I want the best for Pojack, and maybe this is the way to do it. But it could be that I'm wrong... Regardless, as I left Omaha, and found a conscious moment, years later, I began typing this intro. An urge to be ship-shape filled my mind ballasts... Maybe this gun's for Charlie Noble[4]. Should've pointed the thing a long time ago(?).

–   Bradley Angle

---

[4] Charlie Noble: a galley's smokestack, usually brass, on a 15th, 16th, and 17th century sailing vessel. The fastest way to clean Charlie Noble, other than having your cabin boy shine it, is to shoot soft shot through it. Cleaning Charlie Noble is necessary to prevent fires, which are a sure way to die at sea.

TABLE OF YARNS

FOREWORD

> *"A sailor knows too well that his life hangs upon a thread, to wish to be often reminded of it; so if a man escapes, he keeps it to himself, or makes a joke of it." – Richard Henry Dana Jr.*

RICHARD HENRY DANA JR. enrolled for twenty-four months of seafaring aboard a 19th century fur trading ship. Coming from a well-off family, between his sophomore and junior year at Harvard, he set sail for California, via Cape Horn. Over the course of two years he was employed as a sailor – that is, a working-class seaman, who lived in a dark dungeon-like area in the forecastle, before the mast. Dana published his book about ten years later. "Two Years Before the Mast[5]" (Dana, 1840) became a tribute to those who were abused at sea, tortured by their officers, and submitted to the most unnecessary and callous conditions.

Unfortunately for us, Dana missed the mark. As a Harvard man, Dana simply could not relish the life of a ragged sailor. His time at sea was surely full of adventure, hard work, and fear, though it was shielded with deep pockets, friends in high places, and social

---

[5] Before the Mast: prior to the 20th century, "before the mast" was a term used to describe a person's position on a vessel. The working sailor lived in the fo'c'stle of the ship, which is in front of the mast. Today, the term "mast" refers to a non-judicial court martial, or a trial led by the ship's captain. Before the mast could then be meant to mean, in front of the Command for punishment.

standards. Dana's shipmates didn't have these luxuries. *What sailor does?*

Did he help our condition? Dana's message surely contributed to laws and regulations that have come to protect the lives and honor of working sailors, though his portrait in Two Years Before the Mast shows our raggedness as meek. He made the world see us as lowly creatures to be pitied. Dana gave us laws meant to protect our bodies from reckless investors and Ahabs. Though weather-beaten-and-worn seamen don't benefit by donning life-preservers and purchasing sea-lawyer pocket-guides. Shelter from the cabin has created its own problems, and we didn't want protection from the seas. We needed lights in the fo'c'sle.

GRATITUDES

It is only luck that you, or I, were born where and how we were. There is nothing but gratitude in my head for the luck I fell into from the start: Late 20th century America, Middle-Class, Healthy.

- The circumstance for aptitude, intelligence and drive is not ours to claim, it is luck. I am thankful, sort of.
- Each one of my limbs, organs and balls is accounted for.
- My children are healthy, fun, and nearby.
- I am thankful for all those I've encountered at sea. I didn't choose to meet you. I am thankful I did.
- The struggles made me aware. The accomplishments, losses and wins, left me confident, capable, and ready.

The Coast Guard allotted me with experiences and rigging to navigate. The Post 9/11 GI Bill is one of the most palpable tools I've ever received. Thanks to those who made such things possible.

REGRETS

It is only luck that you, or I, were born where and how we were. There is nothing but regret in my head for the luck I fell into from the start: Late 20th century America, Middle-Class, Healthy.

- We live in a world where privilege is rewarded. Privilege should be the reward. But what do I do? Nothing.
- Each one of my limbs, organs and balls hurts or has hurt.
- I regret not contemplating the virtues at a younger age.
- I could have pulled out more.

No thanks to those who use the VA as a pawn in their political scheme. Too many of my OTH brothers die inside, and on the streets, every goddamned, mother fucking, day...

- Pojack Ashore.

A letter to the VA

Pojack Ashore
1399 Webster St.
Alameda, CA. 94501

01/26/2019

DECISION REVIEW OFFICER,

I've heard doctors and nurses whisper through canvas partitions: "They're just looking for handouts." Continuous episodes of The Price is Right in the waiting rooms, detached men staring into their palms, scratching their skin. Who has a reason to think anyone gleefully-skips into this process? This entire sequence, from start to now, has been exactly what I was told it would be. A game. A hassle...

You can jump to conclusions, but remember that roughly 20 veterans a day die of suicide, 8000 since I applied for benefits. Well, 20 a day is what the VA said last year. But we know that figure is extrapolated from shit data. The VA relies on third party data to gain information on over 50% of the veteran population. For the suicide info, the VA settled with the scanty info given by a handful of states. The truth is, no one has accurately documented the social and behavioral characteristics of today's veterans... But don't worry. I won't kill myself any time soon.

Haha. So serious all of a sudden.

Over a year of waiting, and I finally heard back: "DENIED." The VA says I provided "Insufficient Documentation." Though your application form gave a one-inch box to explain disability issues. Disgruntled doctors asked boiler-plate questions. The VA requests and decides cases based on minimal information, while it completely overlooks the massive data analysis it conducts, then it says "Insufficient Documentation..." So then, please allow this document (starting on the previous page through to the end of the book) to serve as Item Nine, on the Appeal to the Board of Veterans' Appeals Form. I hereby request a review of my denied VA Claim.

What follows is a Coastie's confession, which can't fit on your small fucking questionnaire. If you don't read it, maybe someone will... I was healthy when I enlisted in the Coast Guard. Excited when I left boot. Tossed like chum to a soured seawolf. Fought the seas on my own. Followed every fucking order with blind obedience. Was hung out to dry, stiffly on the mast... I was not healthy when I received my discharge. My medical record states this clearly.

Let's back track for a moment... "Veterans are heroes." What a ridiculous proposition. Placing a categorical marker, like "Veteran," on an individual makes sense in some situations. Taking an extremely presumptuous and precise attribute and assigning it to all members of that category is simply not a healthy thing to do. Let me parade your ass down the roads of life with some cheap hero-brand on your personal and unshakable identity. What's special about the entire veteran group? Your parades are for politicians, not veterans, and it makes me bitter! There are undoubtedly many veterans out there who've had tremendous and terrifying experiences in their line of work. I won't compare mine; it was by no means combat threatening. It did not include war-zone episodes of pro-longed traumatic stress, and it did not leave me with missing limbs or organs. Of course some fit the bill of being a "hero." But I am not a hero, and I gag a little bit each time I hear the term. Regardless, I'm not asking to be fucking hero-saluted. We had a contract. If I left in a worse off condition, then I'd be reimbursed for it.

TABLE OF YARNS

We are all humans here. The ideals of "pride," "honor," and "devotion" don't dissolve under the human condition. Every fucking human on this earth has pride, honor and devotion. Every one. We all bounce off of personalities and positions; some of us were born more elastic than others. My memory isn't complete, so my journal has filled in the blanks, and, maybe, so can that ironically thick medical file you keep on your desk.

● ● ●

SHIPMATES

PART ONE

The Thrill

*So quiet, too, was the sea, and so steady the breeze,
that if these sails had been sculptured marble they
could not have been more motionless. Not a ripple
upon the surface of the canvas; not even a
quivering of the extreme edges of the sail, so
perfectly were they distended by the breeze. I was
so lost in the sight that I forgot the presence of the
man who came out with me, until he said (for he,
too, rough old man-of-war's-man as he was, had
been gazing at the show), half to himself, still
looking at the marble sails, — ``How quietly they do
their work!"*
— Richard Henry Dana Jr.

SHIPMATES

YARN 1

MR. B

I WAS JACKED[6]! The Company Commander (CC)[7] said "Ashore" and "378" in the same sentence, and at that moment the outside world drifted away. An adventurous daydream descended into my field of view, leaving a circle of sitting shipmates behind. *Rolling seas went to wrack and ruin upon the mighty prow, submersing the fo'c'stle in muddled spray of foam and sea. Colossal black clouds on the horizon. Wind, salt and angry sky. A group of 19th century sailors shouting over the thunder, as our vessel approached the surreal storm. I was ready with a thick manila line and excitement...* The CC gave an order and subconsciously my body arose to a standing position. *Back to this reality.* The circle of Seaman Recruits[8] were in the process of standing too. We had been sitting on the barracks' floor, receiving orders to our next duty stations. Two more days of basic training and then we were free to show the Guard what we were made of. There wasn't a face among us without a grin.

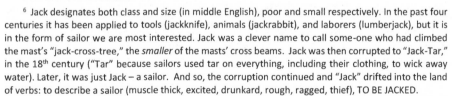

---

[6] Jack designates both class and size (in middle English), poor and small respectively. In the past four centuries it has been applied to tools (jackknife), animals (jackrabbit), and laborers (lumberjack), but it is in the form of sailor we are most interested. Jack was a clever name to call some-one who had climbed the mast's "jack-cross-tree," the *smaller* of the masts' cross beams. Jack was then corrupted to "Jack-Tar," in the 18th century ("Tar" because sailors used tar on everything, including their clothing, to wick away water). Later, it was just Jack – a sailor. And so, the corruption continued and "Jack" drifted into the land of verbs: to describe a sailor (muscle thick, excited, drunkard, rough, ragged, thief), TO BE JACKED.

[7] Company Commander: Also known as the Drill Instructor. The guy at boot camp who yells at you every moment of each day.

[8] Seaman Recruit: The lowest rank in the USCG – E1

Chin parallel to the deck, toes 45 degrees apart. *I'm standing at attention.* "Shit." The orders stated bluntly: DO NOT DRESS IN UNIFORM. My head bent, disgusted I'd failed at the simplest task: to avoid unwanted attention. With a drooping head, a smudge tarnishing my shiny black boots caught my eyes. Like an autonomous robot, my hand went to fix the indiscretion. *Fuck!* Attempting to regain confidence, I slouched, and reached deep in my pocket, feeling for something to occupy my thoughts.

The original communications I had with the 378 foot cutter[9] the "Thrill," stated to report to Small Boat Station San Diego and await further orders. At that temporary duty station, I had received an envelope that included directions and flight itinerary. By the baggage carousel in the Acapulco International Airport, those directions are what my hands found as I pocket jerked for peace of mind.

S.A. J. ASHORE

- DO NOT ARRIVE IN UNIFORM
- Do not tell anyone you are in the Coast Guard
- Do not speak about the Coast Guard
- A prearranged taxi will be waiting outside of your baggage pickup area.
- Good Luck! And WELCOME ABOARD!

A large army-green duffel bag, letters "SA J. ASHORE" stenciled perfectly on the side, spilt onto the baggage claim. Snaking closer and closer to me, standing there, again at attention, with a head buzzed by a number-zero hair trimmer. My sigh was probably audible to everyone within a ten-foot radius.

---

[9] Cutter: in this sense, a Coast Guard ship which has living quarters and berths aboard.

Yelling out of his window, I hadn't even made the taxi platform, "Thrill? You go to Thrill?" He was looking at me. The first symptoms of anxiety pulsed behind my forehead. For weeks I'd been eager to report to my ship, nerves weren't expected to be a part of this. But entering the foreign taxi, the world contracted. "Nervous" would be an understatement.

An opportunity to deliberately breathe presented itself on the ride. I'd never been to Mexico. The taxi rushed through jungle, and every so often a gap in the thick trees would allow for a view of the ocean and harbor below. You could see through the turquoise, to the bleached sand beneath. Then the forest would swallow the view again. Twenty minutes into the ride we descended into the city. Mexican children on each street corner, begging at my window. "Don't give nothing," the driver said. "Desaparecer!" he shouted. "You in Coast Guard? You on big ship?" He glanced at me in the rearview mirror.

I had no answer for the guy, and the question brought on worries. "I am going to the Thrill," I said, avoiding his question, observing the lean and predatory children.

The taxi stopped on a waterfront street. A janky gate was guarded by two armed Coasties. My taxi driver was waiting for a tip, which never appeared. The Coast Guardsmen approached as the taxi peeled away, "Seaman Ashore?"

I looked at their collars, saw they were petty officers. "Yeah, that's me."

"Walk to the end of the pier. You see that guy down there? That's Stagger Lee. He'll check your i.d. and direct you where to go from here. Things are about to get pretty crazy around here, but don't worry about it. You'll be alright." He grinned.

Nerves had solidified to worries, sitting heavy in my stomach. *What did he mean things are going to get crazy?* Walking down the pier I was beside the Thrill, taking notes as I walked. White paint, rust everywhere. 76mm cannon on the bow, 25mm on the 02 deck. A 50cal on the 02 deck with an ammo can in place, though no one manning it. The boat looked like a militant research vessel, odd in a tourist ridden port. At that point in time, the Thrill was huge to me. Guys at Boot said she was manned with 120 sailors (officers included) and could push 30 knots[10].

An armed non-rate with opaque sunglasses in place of eyes, Seaman Stagger Lee, checked my i.d. again. He directed me to the helo-hangar, to await the OOD[11]. As I walked away I could hear him say "he's here," followed by "copy," from a radio. Minutes went by as I stood in a quasi-attention stance, still in my civvies[12]. Another non-rate[13] appeared and explained he was sent by the OOD to help me find my way.

Without any sort of introduction or explanation, our first and only stop was in a dark lounge area. A small group of uniformed guys were watching The Sopranos. The non-rate whispered in my direction without looking, "let me finish this one season then I'll give you the grand tour. There's not much to see, really." He jumped over the couch in front of us and left me standing, once again in an awkward attention pose. *What the Fuck.*

The 1MC[14] broke the silence and everyone sat up. "All-hands on-duty, muster on the mess-deck. Repeat, all hands to the mess deck."

I grabbed my escort by the shoulder as he tried to dart past me. "Oh, sorry man. I've got to go. Just ask a BM[15] what to do." The room became empty, just me and the Sopranos. My knotted stomach twisted further into a ball of confusion, and my thoughts couldn't articulate what I wanted.

---

[10] Knot: Nautical Mile an Hour. The "ship's log" used to be an actual log, thrown overboard with a line attached around it. The line was knotted every few feet. The time it took the log to drift and pull X number of knots, away from the ship, could be used to roughly calculate speed (and drift). Thus, the etymology of "knot" and "ship's log."

[11] OOD: Officer of the Deck. Not necessarily the Captain or Master of the ship. The OOD is the on-duty person in charge of a ship. The Captain takes this role the second he is present.

[12] Civvies: Civilian dress. Regular street clothes.

[13] Non-rate: a low-level enlisted person without a rating. Someone without a specific job. Boat bitch.

[14] 1MC – 1st main circuit. Shipboard public address system.

[15] BM: Boatswain's Mate. A sailor skilled in vessel operations.

There I was, in a dark room, finally aboard the Thrill, listening to a television alone: "You know, Tony, it's a multiple choice thing with you. 'Cause I can't tell if you're old-fashioned, you're paranoid, or just a fucking asshole" (Burgess, 2006). An extremely loud horn started blowing outside. *Shit.*

Back through the passageways, the way I came in, I rushed to the helo-hangar. People were hurrying in every direction. No one paid any attention to me. Stagger Lee was still by the gangway, standing in a relaxed and confident gait. I headed his way. He informed me that the horn was the recall horn, and it notified all of the crew on shore to return to the ship. "We just made a drug bust, and the captain is anxious about the ship sitting here with tons of coke on board." Apparently, the captain set security watches and recalled everyone as soon as the food stores were loaded and fuel replenishments had been made. *Cool.*

"What do I do?"

"Go to your muster station and wait there." He took off to meet an official looking guy on the gangway before I could ask a question. *Where and what is my muster station?*

U nderway, I pretended to be unphased by the inadequate orientation I'd never been given. A BM3 approached me on the fantail[16], where I had found a group of non-rates smoking. Without an introduction he began running through a list of tasks I'd be required to do within my first month. "Stay away from the shitbags and you'll be fine." He stated, without ever looking me in the face. "By the way. Which berthing area are you in? I hope they

---

[16] Fantail: the aft portion of the vessel, which, depending on organization specific vernacular, can encompass the working area on the back of a ship.

didn't put you with those fucking Engineers." I told him I didn't know where my rack was.

"What do you mean? Where's all your stuff?"

"I left it in the crew lounge, where I checked in."

"Wait. What? Who checked you in?"

"I never got his name. A non-rate. Took me to the lounge and left me there once the recall horn blew."

The BM3 grimaced. "God damn it. Wait here." He walked off.

I lit another cigarette.

He came back a minute later and said I'd be staying in the Engineer's Berthing. "Go ahead and find an empty rack in there now, then be on the mess-deck for watch at 2315. If anyone gives you shit, just give it back." He lit a cigarette and waited for me to say something. I was speechless and an awkward silence let the sound of the sea intrude into our conversation.

Pressed uniform and stomach pains, I was on the mess deck by 2300. It was surprisingly busy. Deep-fried imitation mozzarella sticks were being served. "Mid-Rats[17]" I later learned. A deckie[18] introduced himself, "Hey, are you the new guy? I'm Rhyile. You'll be my break-in on helm tonight."

"Oh cool. Just tell me what to do and I'll do it."

"Haha. Scuttle that excitement new guy. You'll just sit and point the stick at whatever number they tell you. It's pretty stupid. We'll go up once the BMOW gets here. Smoke 'em if you got 'em."

"What's the Bee-MŌ?"

---

[17] Mid-Rats: A meal served at mid-night, often reserved for the incoming and outgoing watch only. Abbreviated Midnight Rations.

[18] Deckie: a member of deck-force.

"Boatswain's Mate of the Watch."

There was a door on either side of the galley that led to the exterior walkway on the main deck. I choose the one where no people were congregating. When I latched the door behind me, the ocean took me by surprise. A silent blackness surrounded the ship. A rush of warm wind made my face smile. Alone with the humid night and sparkling cosmos. Under my feet, the ship was plowing away phosphorescent clouds of sea. I lit a cigarette. Leaned on the rail. Put my foot on a chock.

It was my first solitude experience at sea. No sign of life existed anywhere nearby. Behind me, steel bulkheads. To my left and right, a dark walkway. Above and below, more steel decks. Forward, the sea, the sky, with no boundary separating the two. The sound of the ship moving through the dark sea. My mind was quiet. My mind is never quiet.

My cigarette wasn't half gone when Rhyile appeared behind me. "There you are. The BMOW is ready."

"We're all here, might as well go up," was the BM3's logic to start our shift. We (the watch-relief[19]) left the mess-deck for the bridge. One silent ladder after another, through the dark passageways, illuminated red, my nervous thoughts distracted by unfamiliar objects flickering with reflective tape. We climbed towards the bridge, forward without speaking. I took up the rear. One last, lightless, steep and skinny ladderway, and the BM3 knocked on a door, then creaked it open. He nearly shouted: "Request permission to be about the bridge," pulling me out of my

---

[19] Watch-Relief: the individuals readying to relive the current watch standers.

silent thoughts. Mimicking my shipmates, I put a salute on my forehead as I arrived on the bridge for the first time.

There, in the glowing darkness of the bridge, three or four stories above deep black ocean water, I stood at perfect attention as the watch-standers exchanged information. A month out of Basic Training, my ability to stand at attention, salute, and say "yes Sir!" was at an all-time high. And as I did that, I perceived the many pieces of equipment and people around me. It was whelming and I focused on standing stiff.

Once the ritual was finished, Rhyile led me off the bridge to a ladder, and we climbed. "We'll stand lookout first, then, in about an hour, we'll come back down for helm."

On the flybridge[20] a girl emerged from around the mast. She looked at my eyes and smiled, "hi."

Rhyile seemed annoyed: "Lois! Are you going to give me the pass down or what?"

"Oh sorry. The shore is behind us, about 30 miles. There are a few fishing boats back there too. No other contacts." She pressed into me as she moved by us and disappeared down the ladder.

For an hour I stood in awe of my position. Freedom and power were present from that vantage point, in the dark Pacific. Stared at the sea, the stars, where they met. Rhylie seemed unwilling to talk about work. The BM3 soon relieved us back down to the bridge, to switch watches with the helmsmen. It was my turn to take the helm! To drive the boat. Serious was my eighteen-year-old attitude. Thankful to be doing something significant with my life.

[20] Flybridge: the highest area of a ship one can walk (not located on a mast), where a lookout would stand watch.

Whenever we arrived on the bridge to take the helm there was a new Officer of the Deck. There, in a tall skinny gait, stood Mr. B. Quietly he was staring into the blackness of the ocean, and then down, into his mug. Back and forth, I noticed out of the corner of my eye, as I was debriefed on my duty at the helm. *I got this.*

I had two courses to steer by, a gyro course and a magnetic course. Each was numerically different, though directionally the same. A curiosity I cared not about at that time. A stool in front of the helm was restricted for use by qualified personnel only, so I stood and held the helm tight. The slightest movement turned hundreds of tons of ship. The BM3 ordered me to report my heading to the OOD. I was briefed on how to do this, and I spoke to Mr. B. for the first time, relaying the course he already knew we were steering. "Sir. Steering 1-8-5. Sir. Magnetic 1-9-3. Sir." That being done, and Mr. B. saying nothing of my report other than "copy," I stood and looked down at my instruments and commenced steering a course. *Quiet.*

Rhyile leaned silently on the radar beside me and said little, as he was either a shitty instructor or there was little to teach, or something else. I didn't know, but I felt too uneasy to ask. There were gadgets everywhere. A faint smell of musky hungover people. A quartermaster[21] bent over a chart, making marks under a red lamp. The radar screen scanned. The BM3 stepped into the bridge, "all clear about the decks." The doors on either side of the bridge were left open – we were in the tropics in the summer. It was musky, hot and dark. Peaceful. *Quiet.*

Mr. B. interrupted the dark glow of the bridge. "Ashore, is it? Is that pronounced A-Sure or Ashore?"

---

[21]Quartermaster: QM. The official log keepers and navigators aboard a ship. QMs have merged into the BM rating (in the CG), which caused a lot of animosity amongst those with that rating.

There was no time to answer.

"Hey A-sure. Do you know why someone would wrap a hamster in duct-tape?"

I stiffened in my seat. An awkwardness descended around me. The helm I was holding was being held tighter. My eyes moved quickly around the bridge, embarrassed and cowering faces covered in the flickering cast of dim red lights. Rhylie's finger was poking at my shoulder, tapping me, to get me to respond. *Shit.*

"Uh, No. No sir, I don't sir." My reply, showed signs of discomfort, though it made an appropriate effort to speak to my superior in proper tone and order.

"Eh. heh-he," he spoke and laughed like a weasel, "Anyone? Anyone know why you wrap a hamster in duct tape?"

We all looked around to heads nodding "no," looking at the floor with forced smiles.

Mr. B. answered his question so no one was spared. "It's so it doesn't pop when you fuck it."

YARN 2

BM3 JACK KURTZ

N ew guys are pipelined[22] through meetings with their chain-of-command and with department heads, each person giving a full dose of their personality. The BM1, BMC and 1LT[23] cornered me and quickly explained work orientation and rudimentary customs and procedures, each with a helping of witticism that made me silently question their legitimacy.

The Captain's quarters had a makeshift waiting room with a couch, where I sat at attention while the busy Captain bellowed "welcome aboard" so loudly I was startled. I could only see his shadow, silhouetted on a fabric partition that separated his bed and office from the view of the waiting area. "We've been busy, obviously, and I hope to have a longer one-on-one with all of my shipmates in the future." His voice went from loudly passionate to more and more faint with each word. "Also, I have an open-door policy so if you..." he mumbled something and became so quiet the exchange was inaudible and I missed the rest of his policy.

The XO[24] warned about poor hygiene. The EO said not to touch anything. The FSC[25] gave me a run down on chow times. Then I was

---

[22] Pipeline Training: quickly going through mandatory meetings and training to meet the requirements of a new position or unit.

[23] 1LT: The First Lieutenant is a position on a vessel and not a rank. This position is under the Operations Officer and has charge of Deck-Force.

[24] XO: Executive Officer. The second in command.

[25] FSC: Food Service Chief.

off to the DCC, an experience I've recorded later. And finally, my berthing-area petty officer, Boatswain's Mate 3rd Class Kurtz.

Kurtz led me to the deck-force[26] berthing-areas, Hotel California and Margaritaville, and demonstrated his leadership ability once we got there: he pointed to a rack and said to keep my shit clean. "If you stay out of my way, I'll stay out of your way. You'll be moving into Margaritaville in a few weeks."

M argaritaville had fourteen racks, including four 3-highs and a 2-high. Combined, there towards the front of the ship, just before the mast, lived a majority of the seamen, with their two berthing-area petty officers – both BM3s, Kurtz and JJ.

Space was limited in these living quarters. In Margaritaville, my long-term home was the top rack of a 3-high. Located just inside the entrance, it was situated where I'd be blasted with light and noise each time someone opened either the head or the main door. The space in front of my rack was a gap no larger than the width of an adult gorilla – about 2' by 6', the overhead about 7' off the deck. Built into the racks were horizontal lockers, on which a 3" pad rested.

The crew of Margaritaville were all old-timers. After Kurtz, a gang-like group of friends made sure I knew my place. Stagger Lee, Legit and Ray made the space feel more like a holding cell than a berthing area.

---

[26] Deck-Force: a department aboard ship containing boatswain's mates and non-rates, focused on operational activities (launching small boat, painting, mooring, anchoring, more painting, chasing rust, painting again.)

YARN 3

DCC

A loud short man with the mission to save the boat from sinking. Everything was a threat to our boat, according to our bouncy Damage Control Chief. Everything that didn't sink was a fire hazard. Every non-rate, a moving disaster in need of abuse. He stood with a ridiculous sea-stance, four feet wide; he was only five feet tall. We were two days out from Acapulco and I was still ignorant of ship life. The Chief in front of me was the last signature I needed on my orientation list, and he took me directly to the fantail to introduce himself. The ship hardly swaying, only a few degrees, judging by the massive seawhiz[27] behind him. His hands animated his voice, wild and passionate.

He introduced me to each and every fire-station[28], halon[29] station, life-boat, and gear locker and he articulated each and every way the boat could sink, burn or explode. He assigned me a five-pound qualification packet and ordered me to have each item memorized and signed off by "one of his guys." "You have to think about the worst-case scenario at every moment on this ship. Are you smoking where you shouldn't be? Is there an egress route nearby? Is there adequate ventilation in your work space? If there were a fire, how

---

[27] Seawhiz: A highspeed machine gun capable of shooting incoming rockets, planes, missiles and bombs out of the sky. Looks like an over-sized R2D2 with a machine gun penis.

[28] Fire-Station: a location aboard a vessel which has fire-fighting capabilities (fire hose, extinguisher, AFFF)

[29] Halon: Halon is a toxic gas(chemical) used to quickly put out fires in engine spaces.

would I respond? Put it out? Give the signal? What? What would you do! By the time you leave this boat, my mission is to make you the safest God Damned Fucking Coastie out there. There's no room for fuck ups at sea!" He lit a cigarette while glaring at me.

"Look. If you prove yourself to be a hard worker, and you want to get away from those deck apes, you know, those friends of yours who chase rust and paint for a living, I'll pull you over to the Engineers. I'm always looking for quality guys. You look mechanically natured. You aren't scared of hot tight spaces are you?"

I shook my head and started at an answer, "Wow thanks Chief! But I think I want to be a Boatswains—"

He bitterly cut me off. "Look. You fucking deckies always think you know best. Well I'll tell you something. It's the engineers that make these boats perform. Not the boatswain mates, not the god damned officers, not the cooks. You think a cook is going to make a 12-cylinder engine run for three months straight? That's 36,000 horse power bud!" He took a huge inhalation of his smoke and gestured for me to light one up too. His voice went up in pitch and volume. "This reminds me. You fucking deckies think you're so smart. But you can't close a fucking water tight door correctly. If I catch you improperly securing a water tight door or hatch, I'll make your life hell."

As he barraged me with his ego-trip, over my innocent comment about wanting to be a Boatswain's Mate, I pretended he was a little naked midget clown. I fabricated a rainbow wig and inserted it on his head as he lectured.

He kept gesturing for me to join him in a cigarette. I lied and said I didn't smoke.

JOURNAL ENTRY

(October 2002) My energy level is crushed. Nothing is what I expected. At this point, I am writing it all off as an isolated situation, literally isolated! So many angry... Disgruntled... Lazy Assholes.... It'll get better. It'll get better. IT WILL GET BETTER. Benefit of the doubt, right?/! These guys have been at sea for some time. Maybe I'd be like them too.

The perfectly transparent water of Acapulco Bay is stuck in my head. It had zero reflective qualities, like vodka with backwash...

My first lookout watch was good. From the flybridge you could see for 50 miles plus. The stars. The horizon. The sounds and wind. It's where I want to be... Leaving Acapulco we passed by a huge lighthouse and from the flybridge tonight you could see it flash in the distance. My mind overlays my mother's lighthouse – the one at the end of the driveway. That fucking plastic lawn ornament, every day, dragging tracks in the gravel, kicking rocks, walking home, flashless.

YARN 4
SEAMAN STAGGER LEE

"Man, all these clowns, running up and down, round and around! Haha. Man, if you fuckers would just chill."

A dvice from Stagger Lee's mouth, as he crawled on hands and knees cleaning the berthing area. Decked out in PPE, blue latex gloves, dust mask, dark sunglasses, sharp uniform.

Stagger had been on the boat for years, three or four maybe. Always full of energy, smoker, apparently liked by the 1LT. He was one of the alpha males in the berthing area: between him, Kurtz and Legit. I watched him closely when I first arrived to the boat. There was something there I could not relate to. A cultural thing that I missed in my youth perhaps. Something else? *Energy?* Style?

YARN 5

LEGIT, SEAMAN

Someone had music blasting during the fight. That fucking song that wouldn't stop. "I'm sorry Ms. Jackson. I am for real." The engineers had teamed up with the cooks and had entered Margaritaville like they were a swat team. In a moment of seconds our berthing area went from a relaxing lounge, most of us in our racks, the usual gang playing Xbox, to a pile of sweaty dudes yelling, wrestling and taking cheap cracks on each other in a dog pile.

These fights were becoming more regular and more intense as the patrol went on. The boat was split into groups, divided first by division, deck-force vs engineering, and then by berthing area. Sometimes the divisions weren't so clear. The main point was to burn off testosterone, I speculate. For this specific fight, our fellow deck-force members, from Hotel California, had previously negotiated a truce with the engineers. This meant that Margaritaville was greatly undermanned: there were 14 of us and 20 or more of them. Outkast was still playing as we fought: "Never meant to make your daughter cry. I apologize a trillion times."

A punch landed in my side and made me curl into a ball. I was on the bottom of the pile. Six or more bodies on top of me. Yells increasing in volume. A burst of anger came from high on the pile: "Who the fuck just hit me?" Someone was throwing painful jabs. Aggression was building and the quasi-fun dog pile was getting heated. From the bottom, I could see through the limbs and bodies and saw Ray (Seamen) on Tikki's (Fireman) back, throwing jabs into the back of his head. Tikki slammed all of his 220lb body back into a locker, and Ray's body arched as it hit a coat hook. More screaming. I felt space generate under me and I reacted with my feet, placed them under me and shot straight up, throwing people off me as I went. I dove across the room and grabbed Tikki's belt and ripped him down. I was on the bottom of a pile again instantly, this time flattened like roadkill with my chest unprotected. But my left fist was exposed and I went for any fireman I could see.

An authoritative voice was in the background: "Cut it out! Quit this shit now!" The pile on top of me started to lighten. More rustling and more shouting. Legit and Ray had cornered Tikki in a corner and were threatening him. Tikki was a gigantic mass of muscle from Hatti. Him and Legit, both huge black dudes, made Ray look like Rudy, from the Notre Dame football team. Tikki looked like he wanted to kill someone. Ray and Legit were about to attack him. I was making my way for the three to join the fun. Legit raised his arm to throw a punch and his elbow caught me in the face in the process. My instincts weren't the best: "What the fuck, Boy!"

He took me to the floor in a flash and was on top of me. A knife-hand in my face. "What'd you call me?"

The room had stopped. "My baby's drama mama, don't like me She be doing things like having them boys come from her neighborhood!" blaring on the stereo.

I could sense the eyes on me. Legit was staring at my face. I could throw him off, but I need to diffuse the situation. *Fuck. I'm I going to get masted for being a racist.*

"I said, what'd you call me?"

Ray was piping in. "What'd he call you man? What's up Legit?"

"He knows what he called me."

For centuries, both the British and American Navies used the term "boy" to mean, "unqualified seaman." i.e. Cabin-boy. This tradition lasted all the way through the beginning of the 20th century. "Boy" is also a term white racist use to refer to black people.

JOURNAL ENTRY

(November 2002) Made it back. Wanted to stay longer.

Clark said he would buy me a 1/5 of Jack, said that I'd be wise to load up on Robotusin too, because that was the last time he'd buy me booze.

The HS Chief said there wouldn't be any opening in the barracks for a few months, and I, as a new guy, would have to live on the boat for a few deployments first, before being eligible for the barracks.

The second we hit port everyone scattered. A group of deckies said they were going to pregame in the barracks and said I could come along. The barracks turned out to be a twelve-story building about a mile from the boat, still on the Navy base. I expected some sort of order. There wasn't any.

About 10 of us were crammed in a little room and there was an endless supply of cheap beer. Within hours of pulling into San Diego, I couldn't walk. Instead I stumbled back to the boat, in the cover of darkness, and managed to crawl back into my rack.

YARN 6
GEORGIA, SEAMAN APPRENTICE

Labels based on character, personality, deeds or looks are common on ships. Jack London based each and every one of his characters off of a socio-political emotion. Melville's characters on the Pequod were symbolic of dogma, personality and culture. Mark Twain's, America's classic personalities (he didn't make the classics, he just did the obvious thing and put them in prose). Dana conspicuously left out the characters of his shipmates, with the exception of the "handsome sailor," who Melville later borrowed.

Georgia was from somewhere in the South, had an accent, and was thick and hairy. As the Thrill pulled into San Diego, from the Acapulco deployment, Georgia and a group of other newbies were standing by on the quaywall[30]. Within a day, the lot of us were placed on mess-cooking[31] detail, where we bitch-worked for the cooks for a month.

Messcook duty would start at 0445, underway or in port. This was to help the cooks begin prepping for breakfast, which was served at

---

[30] A quay is the area of a pier-structure which is perpendicular to the pier/dock fingers. The quaywall, specifically, is the physical wall that divides land from water. Note that a dock floats, a pier is not affected by tides.
[31] Mess-Cooking: the lowest position on a ship. Duty assigned to serve the needs of the cooks (scullery maid, deep sink, wardroom attendant, etc)

0600 each day. A messcook's first task each day is to clean up mid-rats, from the night before. Next is to carry the cook's food list from storage to the galley – one order from the refer and a second order from dry-stores. Dry-stores was located in the fo'c'sle below the boatswain's hole[32]. The refers were located in the rear of the vessel below aft berthing. Each order, for each meal, would require a few boxes from each location. This could take about an hour of slumping heavy, cold, broken boxes across the length of ship. Due to a 15-foot ladder, dry-stores required at least two people. This is where Georgia and I spent his first month on the ship. With the right attitude and skill, a trip to dry-stores could be extended to last a few hours. Georgia and I mastered the art of dry-stores shit-bagging[33] quickly. We spent hours each day, during work routine, talking about music and the South, relaxing. It was a rite of passage.

"Willie is good man, though some of his shit sucks. You know that gospel shit he does. Man, I could never get into that shit. Jerry Garcia plays some good gospel music. Whewwww! Goddamned Jerry Garcia! What about old Merle Haggard. You like him? Huh? I like Merle. My pops used to blast nothing but Merle. Hey Ashore. You know who David Allan Coe is? Huh? You don't know who David Allan Coe is? Man, you ain't from the South. You know Virginia's 'bout as North as you can get huh. Hahah. David Allan Coe is the shit. My pops loved him. We used to listen to him everywhere. Aw man. He's got some racist songs out there. You ever here 'Rudolph the Big Lipped Nigger?' or 'Fucked by a Nigger?' Haha. That shit is real country. He's good. Not all of his shit is racist though. He's got some sad

---

[32] Boatswain's Hole: area of ship reserved for projects of the boatswain's mates. Deck-force mustered in the boatswain's hole aboard the Thrill.

[33] Shit Bagging: (Verb) the act of artfully, strategically, or casually not doing work.

bluesy shit too. You got to look him up Ashore. If you say you like Waylon, you'll like Coe. He's the shit."

These conversations would go on from hours to days, and I'd just soak it in. Georgia placed a lot of music in my head. From Country Western to the Grateful Dead, to Warren Haynes... The influence people have over us.

Georgia and I also shared drug stories:

"Man you did too much acid. I never touched that shit. In Atlanta we had the 'tweet-tweet.' You know what the 'tweet-tweet' is Ashore. God Damn. Wheewww! Snort that shit. Smoke that shit. Pack that shit in the gums. God Damn! Hey Ashore. You ever go to TJ. I heard they got some cocaine down there that will make your blood boil. Wheeew! God Damn. Let's go get some 'tweet' brother. Wheeew! Tweet, tweet. Tweet, tweet!!!!

YARN 7

SEAMAN COOLK

We were mustering one morning in the bosun's hole. Mr. B. about to take center stage, when Seaman Coolk made a grand and loud entrance, through the 8-dog[34] water tight door. We all turned as we heard the first dog rotate open; the others quickly followed. Coolk walked in, closing fast the door behind him, dogging down each dog, the bottom right dog hanging loose because the wedge lost its rubber long ago. His face was marked with a purple bruise that encompassed his entire left cheek and most of his eye socket.

Coolk: "Sorry I'm running a little behind this morning Chief. Mr. B. Sorry."

Mr. B: "What the fuck does this look like Coolk? A bed and breakfast? Can I make you some pancakes? How about a smoke and a pancake Coolk? Eh Coolk? Eh Rhylie, how's about a smoke and a pancake for Coolk?

Coolk: "Oh sir, I've got a story."

Mr. B cut him off: "Nobody cares Coolk. You're late. BM1. Talk to Coolk about this after muster. What Coolk? Someone give you the reach around? Hehahe. The old reach around?"

"No shit sir. I was beat up by some tranny hooker in TJ last night."

---

[34] Dog: opposite a cat, also, a rotating lever on a water-tight door or hatch, used to compress the door to the bulkhead. Commonly used doors would have a quick-acting handle, which would close all dogs in one motion.

There was a pro-longed moment of silence. *Did underage Coolk just admit to going to Tijuana last night? Did he just confess to buying a tranny hooker?* What the fuck?

Mr. B.'s face was caught off guard, but his dirty mind didn't miss a beat. BMC and BM1 looked to the ground. Stagger made the only noise: "oooh!"

"Coolk, I said nobody cares... unless there is a part about a reach around. You give it or get it Coolk? The old reach around?" Mr. B's face slowly turned into one of intrigue and genuine excitement.

Coolk: "We got a booth and she was talking about money. When she took off her pants I noticed a bulge in her panties and when she caught me staring she hit me right here with her elbow." He pointed to the wrong side of his face. "I fell down confused and put my arms over my head. Then that fucking transvestite started peeing on me. I covered myself and curled up, and when the piss stopped, I looked up and she was gone. She stole my fucking wallet."

The BM1 grabbed Coolk's arm, "Alright Coolk. That's enough. Come with me."

Seaman Gabriel stood up to plead some sort of case for Coolk, but we didn't get to hear it because he hesitated long enough to silence himself and sit back down.

The BM1 led Coolk back through the water tight door, eight dogs open, seven dogs closed, one hanging loose. We listened and watched the movement of each one.

Mr. B: "I bet he got the reach around."

YARN 8
STAGGER LEE, SN

White glove inspection. The door was cracked open. I could see Stagger in the head on his hands and knees. He scrubbed the corners of the deck, where it met the bulkhead, with a toothbrush. Back and forth at an unnatural speed. A paper dusk mask and sunglasses covered his face. Scalp perfectly shaved, reflective, just like the linoleum deck.

In a flash, he went from his crawling position to standing up. He faced himself, leaned in so far his mask started bending inwards on the mirror. He leaned back and removed the annoying object and exposed a double layer of pristine white perfectly in-line teeth. He put his brush under the faucet, then to his teeth, with a deliberate and precise stroke, back and forth, faster than before. He stopped suddenly and froze. A prolonged moment. He removed the brush and pushed his sunglasses to his forehead. He was staring at my eyes, by way of the mirror. It took me seconds to realize I was watching him watch me. My eyes blinked and my forehead contracted then relaxed. He gave a slow-motion wink and kicked the door shut.

No grime was safe from the XO's white glove. Followed by the HSC[35], the XO went from one compartment to the next, inspecting for cleanliness. Each Friday, Stagger arrived ready to go. Excited to outwit the man, toothbrush in hand. This Friday was a bit more intense, as we made preparations to get underway. We were given a two-week notice.

The vibes from people on the boat were a mixture of excitement, anxiety, and despair. Each vibe correlated to a person's family status: loaners were excited; family men were despairing.

Stagger grabbed me one day during muster: "Can I use Ashore for inventory today, Chief?"

We spent hours in the boatswain's cage recording the serial numbers on each of the pneumatic and electric tools. As we went through the list, Stagger prodded me for details about my past.

As the lead seaman on the Thrill, I was a bit cautious to respond accurately to all of his questions. But when he said that Georgia and him were talking about me, I gauged his inquiries were more for his personal protection than for any specific interest.

"I heard you like to party./?"

---

[35] Health Service Chief

YARN 9
BLUEJAY, SEAMAN APPRENTICE

I t was only after the herpes outbreak had taken over his chin that I spoke with him. Before that, he was just some new guy on the boat. At least ten other new people had come, and ten older guys had left. New people lost their novelty. We were all strangers, even as we became intimate with each other, sometimes for years.

He was at the butt of every joke. The herpes outbreak was icing on the already glorious cake. The sea-story of Jay and Bluejay spread like a bravo-fire[36] through the boat. Introduced by Seaman Gabriel, who was a first-person witness, it gained tremendous momentum from Mr. B.

Tijuana is where everyone underage went to party while not on duty. The Thrill homeported in San Diego, 32nd St. Naval Base, amongst most of the Pacific's Naval Fleet. Being so close to the border, it made sense for us to head there to buy booze and whatever else we wanted. We could get alcohol in San Diego, though there would be a surcharge as we would have to pay an older shipmate to buy it for us. Ironically, Bluejay was over the age of 21, but he went to TJ for more important things than alcohol.

It was late one night in Tijuana when Jay and Bluejay met each other. After a long and dirty evening, Bluejay stumbled outside a tourist bordello for a cab to the border.   That's when he ran into Jay and Gabriel. In the awkward and coincidental meeting, the three caught a cab together. Jay and Bluejay jumped in the aft seat of the cab without much thought. Gabriel was in the passenger seat and the

---

[36] Bravo Fire: A fire burning liquid or combustibles for fuel (Gasoline, JP5, Diesel).

cab driver, well, he was in the driver's seat. In the back seat, my sloshed friend Bluejay decided to make a move on Jay. Which turned out to his benefit because she took the attention to heart and sucked his dick in return. All the while, Gabriel and cabbie enjoyed the show. To make things more interesting, the cabbie decided to tilt his rearview mirror towards the backseat and get a good view of Jay's panties, which were nicely displayed between her splayed legs and summer skirt. The cabbie reached for Jay's crotch and started fingering her while he continued to drive with his free hand.

Bluejay received his lifelong nickname the next morning when Gabriel spilled the story to the crew. Mr. B, forever being amongst the yarn, began to refer to the two as a pair of doves. Then to expedite his witticism, simply as Jay and Bluejay. A week later, Bluejay, full of anger and embarrassment, broke out in the worse herpes rash anyone has ever had. It crawled over his face like ivy in a wet rain forest.

JOURNAL ENTRY

We must come down from our heights, [...]see what has been wrought among our fellow-creatures by accident, hardship, or vice.
—Richard Henry Dana Jr. (Dana, 1840)

(January 2003) Today was a shit show. There were family members all over the fucking boat. Seems like half the boat was sitting on their ass, two-facing their wives, as the boys and I fiddle fucked the mooring lines, smoke lamp extinguished. We were late to sea by hours, then had to stop in Point Loma to get our smokes in.

A neighbouring carrier[37] had arrived earlier and the families at that dock were less in number than the families on our boat. Those bastards had been at sea for 6 months. What are we doing? Going to Disney World for a few weeks? Bitch slapping some unlucky Mexican fellas, and returning quasi-heroes? What does the Navy think of us? We moor on their dock

---

[37] Carriers: large naval vessels which act as landing areas for both helicopter and fixed wing aircraft. i.e. Air-Craft Carrier.

scraps, deploy to vacation destinations, and flood the boat with the families of lifers. Their floating cities disappear for half of the year. Crackerjack uniforms and bunnies aboard. They come home to radio salutes and missing wives, parades and newly unwrapped red, white, and blues.

America. Fuck yeah.

YARN 10
GILMOUR, SEAMAN APPRENTICE

Gilmour arrived about the same time Bluejay did. There was nothing there in the beginning that foreshadowed our friendship of 20 years, least not that I recall. Like Bluejay, Gilmour reported with a group of other non-rates. All seamen who would replace my status as one of the new guys.

Gilmour and I first met during a deck-force meeting. These daily musters took place in the boatswain's hole, located on the second deck, the level down from the main deck, in the forward part of the ship. The boatswain's hole is the one place on the ship that a member of deck-force might feel at ease, with some charge. On the Thrill, the deck of the boatswain's hole was painted with a 6' skull and cross bones. It's overhead rose 20' above the deck, where a large removeable hatch allowed cranes to lower ammunitions and dry stores. An amass of different lockers created the perimeter bulkhead: the boatswain's locker was a storage room for deck-force tools; fire-locker #1 was primary mustering spot for general quarter's fire teams; two line[38] lockers were on either side, which included all of the mooring gear for the forward part of the ship as well as deck gear for anchoring and towing evolutions; forward was the sea-chest, which was a locked area where crew were allowed to store personal items for long periods and where crew were not allowed to hide to

---

[38] Line: The only rope you'd find on a ship would be on a spool. Once off the spool rope becomes line. Mooring line, working lines, heaving lines, running lines, etc. Using the term rope around a boatswain's mate is a good way to weed out a person with poor self-management skills.

have sex with fellow shipmates; and then there were two 8-dog-water-tight doors on either side, one led aft to the second deck passageway and one led forward to the hazmat locker and paint locker. The main door, leading aft to the second deck passageway, once was a quick-acting water tight door but the DCC had replaced it so "deckies could learn how to properly dog a door." A meeting in the boatswain hole entailed about 20 to 30 deck-force personnel, all the Boatswain's Mates, the BMC and Mr. B., Deckies would sit in a circle, the newer guys in the middle of the circle, and the petty officers would stand around the circle, leaning against the various bulkheads, lockers and gear. The BMC and 1LT would move about at their discretion.

I sat leaning against fire locker #1 with a horrid hangover, wearing dark sunglass, trying to focus just enough to respond to any order from above. Mr. B was yakking away, showing off for the new guys. Gilmour was sitting in front of me wearing those old janitor looking uniforms we used to wear back when the CG was DOT. I could just make out a Pink Floyd Sickle tattooed on his left shoulder – I knew I had to befriend him.

He was more than a Pink Floyd fanatic. His father had named him after David Gilmour, and his older sister and him had remembered the words to the entire Bob Dylan discography. Gilmour was a third generation Coastie, along with his older sister who was then stationed in Portland. Gilmour's dad worked as a civilian Coastie, writing contracts out of Mobile. Gilmour was not fazed by my abrupt questioning over his tattoo and we were quickly making plans to talk shop over music.

By this time, the Thrill was prepping for another Southern Pacific patrol. My time onboard had exceeded six months and the new guys, especially Gilmour and Bluejay, were looking up to me to answer questions about prepping for sea. "Stock up on cigarettes, even if you don't smoke," was my first line of advice. My second was "they can't test you for Robotusin," and finally "you'll need niacin after the port calls to help detox." I was proud of my knowledge, and I was being a good guy by sharing it - no one bothered to take me under their wing in the beginning.

We set sail once more for the Central American Coast, and were given no other details of our mission. Moving a few hundred miles a day, from San Diego, we were in operation mode by the second week. By week three we had found an Ecuadorian fishing vessel adrift off the coast of Guatemala. There, fifty miles from the nearest coastline, floated a 60' wooden trawler, out of fuel, out of supplies, and with 120 hardly alive Ecuadorian political refugees, crammed into every cranny, awaiting their freedom or death. Our helo had spotted them and it took us at least two days to high-bell to their location. In an effort to manage smells, the migrants had tied their dead to long lines at the end of the trawling booms. The official dead count never made it to the crew, though the number was above a dozen, mostly elder men I heard. As we took them aboard, I learned my first Spanish words. *Una Mas.*

The politics behind this quasi rescue mission I never understood. As we approached a port, which we later found out was Costa Rica, we were informed that our new company would try to jump overboard to avoid being detained. I didn't know where we were and what we were doing, there is no way they did either. And as we anchored in a cove, within a few hundred yards of a beach, we watched as the poor bastards hid their few valuables in their shoes and underwear. It was known that immigrants would be robbed, beaten, abused and raped on their long journey back to their home country. It was also understood that their attempt to flea may be met with draconian law or even death. *Yay, the Thrill!*

And then we went on to our other business, of chasing supposed enemies. This business was arbitrary for us crew, other than it allowed us duties in addition to our daily routine of double watches, helm/lookout, followed by the day-to-day work routine – painting and chasing rust.

We'd often launch a helicopter to extend our eyes. As part of the helo-deck fire team, we would standby[39] in the helo hanger, at the chance of a fire on the flight deck. I'd take my guitar and strum to Gilmour's lyrics. Singing, "Whoo, ho, ho, would you give me a chase please. I'm all jacked up and on my knees. Yo ho ho, I'm all jacked up."

Just like commercial ships, the Thrill often needed to replenish food and fuel. Hitting port in any foreign country comes with a big cost to both the CG's operations and the crew's pockets. If we were lucky, the crew would not know if we were approaching a port-call[40] until the day of, because the excitement made the clock slow. Often both the time and location were classified information and were restricted to specific personnel on the ship. Critical information like length of stay, liberty[41] status, and drinking rules were never confided to the crew until final division musters. The length of stay

---

[39] Standby: to wait for an order.
[40] Port-call: a temporary stay of a vessel while on a prolonged deployment.
[41] Liberty: a period granted to sailors to leave the ship and their duties.

was also a variable of what stores and/or fuels were needed. If we had to replenish everything and take on a truck load of fuel, we would be at the dock for a few days. For certain captains, under certain conditions (like the time I met the Thrill in Acapulco), a Cinderella liberty[42] would be implemented, whereby all crew should be within hearing distance of the ship's whistle and back on the ship by midnight each night. This Cinderella liberty was a good way to quickly get back underway, but it also forced the crew to keep their partying to a minimum. Other captains would initiate drinking restrictions: no drinking, or no drinking if you're under the age of 21. Whatever the case of liberty, the captain was often stuck in a predicament: He would want to return to sea asap, to fulfill the mission (drug runners often had their own intel and they would only send ships up the coast if we were in port), though he also would want to keep his crew under control: too long of stay and his crew could get in trouble, too short of a stay could lead to animosity from the crew. Drinking rules also came with a conundrum: Rules didn't mean shit when you were out of uniform. A captain who issued strict drinking rules was a captain who stayed busy with masts and court marshals – no fun for the officers to deal with all that paper work.

Gilmour and I hit port for the first time together that summer, in Mazatlán Mexico. Once off the ship, about five of us deckies stood on an old run-down corner with our shirts off, scrawny arms in the sun. All of us chain smoked as we savored our first six pack of Modelo. The dirty streets called for us, and we were thirsty for action.

---

[42] Cinderella Liberty: temporary liberty which ends at a specific time, normally midnight. May also have other restrictions, like a distance or alcohol restrictions.

An OS1[43] asked if we'd go in on an 8-ball. And in a drunken moment, I was in a room with about ten people from the Thrill, a mountain of cocaine in the center of us. More on the bed stands. A giant brass bed behind me. A huge rush through my heart, confusion in my head. Gilmour and the 1st talking politics. A bottle of Jack. Scuttlebutt[44] being flung around too fast, I couldn't make sense of it. Then a knock on the door. Someone said, "oh shit its chief." Commotion everywhere. Panic? Scurrying people everywhere, hiding powder and paraphernalia.

Desperation flooded my brain as I thought about getting kicked out of the Guard for drug abuse. With no great spot to hide, I ducked behind the bed and crawled under. Beneath the bed I found a brown woman in nothing but her panties, mascara smears under her eyes. I ran my gaze over her dark skin and pain-stricken face. I put a finger over her lips, "sshhhhhh." We could hear someone enter the room. The party continued. I listened to it all night, watching feet.

I never made the connection between the strange girl quietly crying in her underwear beside me and the reality of the situation I was in. I wanted more coke. My emotions jumped sporadically from fear to laughter. *Where the fuck is Gilmour?* The girl beside me couldn't understand my English whispers, so I took the opportunity to use a joke I'd learned from Mr. B.: "Hey. Hehe. Don't turn this rape into a murder."

My humor was lost on her, and it made me feel sick. The night slowed and the feet became fewer. I couldn't hide any longer and I advanced from my fox hole. The OS1 was staring at me in astonishment, and I walked around him like it was nothing, out into

---

[43] OS1: Operations Specialist. 1 = 1st class which is the 6th rank in the enlisted realm.

[44] Scuttlebutt: first used to describe a person with an ass so big it would not fit through a scuttle (a door opening horizontally through decks). Later it was corrupted to mean water fountain – or a place to group together and gossip about big asses. And eventually it was corrupted again, just to mean gossip.

a hotel hallway, out into the brightness of a day, downhill, towards the water.

G etting underway after a port call requires hard labor for those on mooring detail – me and Gilmour. On the fantail we had two BM3s, one BM1, and the Ops Officer. Sometimes the BMC would come around and shout "Hey Now!," as he walked past. Gilmour and I were one of ten deckies who responded to orders about handling lines.

Our mooring lines could be set up to 150 feet long and they were 3 inches in diameter. They would be hauled in and flaked on deck by man power alone. Once clear of the port we would coil the lines in the line-locker below – a small dark void with no ventilation. The BM3s would pick the deckies who smelled the most of alcohol. Or, if the deckie was smart, he'd volunteer to be in the void – making the BM3's life easier – thus gaining status amongst the higher-ranking crew. We always volunteered.

The line lockers lacked ventilation, and on a tropical summer midday, liquor dripping from your pores, vomiting was not uncommon. Again, to hide the deed of drinking underage, one could not vomit up stale alcohol in front of his superiors. In the line locker void, the stench of stomach vile and moldy mooring lines would often overpower new crew. Gilmour laughed as I hurled in the corner.

YARN 11

FS3 CARRAMAT

W e weren't friends. He would buy booze if I paid for it. We would share.

Underway, we were assigned the same GQ1[45] billet, at the 50 cal station. It was a billet which required standing-by in a flash-hood, smoking cigarettes and making small talk, as the Thrill pushed onwards towards more water, cutting holes in the sea. Drills were almost daily, if not every other day. Again and again, Carramat and I would don our musky fire-retardant hoods, light our cigarettes and say meaningless words. "That's a pretty sunset."

CARRAMAT'S LOVER

It was amazing that he could drive to El Paso and back on a weekend. He'd hit an ice-pipe on a Friday afternoon and he'd race off. On Sunday night, he'd stumble into the barracks having never slept, with stories of his teenage lover. She was seventeen. Her mother acknowledged and accepted their

---

[45] GQ1: General Quarters Station Bill 1. A list of predetermined positions for all crew during specific ship operations.

relationship, so he said. They met during a port call Carramat made on a different ship, in Mexico, and had "fallen in love." Carramat talked about her soft curvy teenage body, mostly. By smoking meth in San Diego, he found the time to make the drive to Texas and back. This short time window and drug habit created a conundrum for Carramat's sex cycle. "It takes me hours to cum," he'd tell me, while he leaned against the railing, smoking. "Haha. She loves me man. Shit her mother loves me. I think I'll marry her and get BAH[46]."

I'd have to pull my flash-hood down around my neck to release the heat build-up. Everything he said after his description of fucking went right by me. As the rest of the crew went through the drill routine, or fire/oil problem, I'd stand there by the 50cal with an erection. Picturing a young blond girl in Daisy Dukes getting railed by my 27-year-old shipmate. Her in love. Him high on methamphetamines.

Tweet. Tweet. Tweet.

---

[46] BAH: Basic Allowance for Housing. A monthly stipend service members are entitled to under certain conditions. BAH amounts can vary from $500 per month to $4000 per month.

YARN 12

LOIS SA

S he was on the fantail, after mooring stations were secured, watching the Central American coastline disappear. A shipmate of ours, Clark, who later was kicked out for repetitive AWOL convictions and reporting drunk to duty, was watching Lois schlep wet line to its stowage locker. Not giving a shit to help, he was chain smoking and giving her harsh criticism about what she should do better. The rest of us were resting against the rail, watching in anticipation of Lois going on one of her fits. She did. Her yells at Clark were met with escalating-jeers:

"Lois, if you would stop worrying about me and just put the line away like a real sailor, you'd be fine."

Lois yelling, "you son of a bitch. Fucking help me. You're not doing anything. Fucking help me."

The white and yellow hats, the supervisors, were getting a kick out of the fiasco as well, and we all looked left and right for popcorn. Soon, Lois's screams turned into cries, and Clark lit another cigarette. Lois swung at Clark, who was able to dodge it easily. Lois pursued, stumbled over the pile of line of the deck, and fell to the nonskid.

"You fucking ass hole," she screamed as she charged him again.

Clark chanted, "Jerry! Jerry! Jerry!" as she attacked with punch after punch. The laughs and taunts from us audience were growing louder. Emotionally hijacked, she threw up her arms and started aft, away from us, to hide from the scene.

Then Ops, "Lois! Get back here and finish stowing that line properly." We all got quiet, watched, lit cigarettes. Clark lit one too. Then Ops.

JOURNAL ENTRY

(February 2003) It's strange to write in here. Each punctuation seems to match the sway of the boat. One period in this trough, one comma on that crest, port, starboard, port, starboard, port, starboard... Where are we swaying to?

While making my way through the officer's deck, I passed by the 1lt's door and overheard him saying we were not going home on schedule...

I've noticed that everyone has shit all over their racks. Photos, Tv, PlayStations. Fucking Stagger has a rice cooker. My rack is empty. Where are my memories. My distractions?

Do guys really cum in their socks?

Stagger said he could get me meth if I was interested.

YARN 13

BM3 SILVER

A scream in the middle of the night: "Daddy don't go!" Startled, I jumped up, bashing my face into the firemain directly above my rack. Confusion. A light came on. *The head light. What the fuck.*

"What the fuck," Legit murmured from his side of the dark berthing area. Quietness. Margaritaville was awake. It took a few moments to realize what had happened. That, BM3 Silver, the new guy on deployment, screamed in his sleep.

The next morning, I overheard Jack Kurtz whisper to Silver. Silver's face fell to a frown. He was walking out of the berthing area when Ray yelled, "Daddy don't leave me!" There was a chuckle from each rack. I felt a grin grow on my face.

YARN 14

SEAMAN DOZER

t was too hot to be outside, above 100 degrees with high humidity. The 1LT hadn't been seen due to some unknown "illness." The BMs had us fucking needle gunning the gun deck, without shade, under the equator sun. The plan was to needle gun the non-skid[47] off on Day 1. Prime on Day 2. And paint on Day 3

On Day 1, there were six of us, blasting Beach Boys, wearing BDUs cut at the knees – hot shorts. The needle gun's violent jackhammering blocked out any chance of hearing the music. The high bulkhead aft of us blocked out any chance of being seen from the bridge[48] above, and the port and starboard water-tight doors prevented a boatswain's mate from flanking us in surprise. We devised a system where one person would needle gun on the far side, opposite the stereo. The other five would enjoy the music, chain smoke, and keep watch on the water tight doors. Dozer was on the needle gun, focused on drawing a dick in the non-skid. Legit, Rhyile, Ray, Lois, Coolk, Bluejay and I were taking turns watching the water-tight door dogs, ready to pounce to work, practicing the art of shit-bagging. Skin browning in the tropic sun and ocean reflection.

Suddenly Dozer yelled and his needle gun stopped. "SHIT!" We all ran over. "I actually managed to needle gun through the hull!" Straight into the boatswain's hole. A small beam of light shone through, about the size of a nickel. We all fingered the steel deck, in awe of its thinness, from years of rust and corrosion, or from cheap build. We didn't know.

---

[47] Non-skid: A two part epoxy mixed with sand to create a non-slippery surface for the deck of ships.
[48] Bridge: An area that encompasses a vessel's helm, pilot house, and other steering stations.

On Day 2, the primer bubbled on the deck and created noxious fumes, which quickly mixed with smoke from our never-ending cigarettes and dissipated. The remnants dried into putty.

On Day 3 we entered the Gulf of Tehuantepec. The bare steel took wave after wave. It would be rusted before we left to calmer waters.

CAPTAIN

> *"Now hear this. We've been waiting for this ladies and germs. Our helo has just reported a go fast 40 nautical miles from our position. It is taking action to intercept them as I speak. This is what we train for. This is what we do. You know what to do. GQ2. I repeat, this is not a drill. GQ2. Ops and staff report to CIC. "*

YARN 15

BLUEJAY, SN

The Coast Guard, and maybe military in general, tries to keep enlisted men on their toes to prevent complacency but also to promote loyalty. If you cannot establish yourself in a community because you move every few years, the organization becomes your community. Your ability to join networks and groups outside the Coast Guard is diminished. Similarly, if you cannot settle, you cannot become complacent. And thus, the Thrill *tries* to alternate her operations, between (1) North to fishery patrols in the Bering Sea and (2) South to drug patrols in the Pacific. It was on my second patrol south, and Bluejay's first, that I became aware of the irony of what we are doing.

There is nothing essentially wrong with cocaine. Like most other recreational drugs, it was outlawed due to the Christian vote – any attempt to alter consciousness is an afront to their existence. It is mistakenly known to cause health problems, it only does so due to the mixture of obscure chemicals dealers cut it with – which would be a non-issue if it were legal and then regulated by the FDA, like alcohol. In its pure form, a large dose can be lethal to your heart, but so can alcohol, Tylenol, and dieting supplements. Cocaine in its pure form is what the Thrill chased off the coast of Central America. Cocaine in its pure form is on the streets in Central America (it's cut with toxins in the USA, and most people here are using crack when they think they are using Cocaine – a big and unnecessary mistake. Also, laboratory drugs like methamphetamines are more common in areas where natural drugs like Cocaine are hard to get). Cocaine in its pure form was the drug of choice for Coasties in port calls in Central America, because it would leave your system in a day or two and not expose you during random drug tests, like marijuana would. Cocaine in its pure form was lining my nasal cavity as I sat in a random room in Puerto Vallarta..

I was examining a beautiful jungle on the glossy laminated pages of some magazine. I was in a lobby or a waiting room, and Bluejay had left minutes or hours before in the back of a pickup truck to get drugs. "Wait here dude. I'll be right back."

The reaction someone with ADHD has to speed is not what you would expect. Like the harder drug Ritalin, cocaine brings focus, clarity and control to the user. It also brings euphoria. My fading focus and dwindling good-sensations snapped my attention to the room I was in and Bluejay's absence. Where am I? Where did Bluejay go? I looked around for a clock, a sign, something. Through the door, the city was booming. Foot traffic, beater cars, cops, sun. *Where the fuck am I? How long have I been here?*

My sense of time was blemished. *How long have I been in this port?* There were people becoming concerned about my presence though no one seemed willing to speak with me, which is good because it would have been in Spanish. I was becoming concerned too. *What will I do if Bluejay doesn't return? Is he ok? Should I leave him? Did he leave me?* I watched people come and go, all looking at me and then quickly looking away. I felt the sweat build up on my forehead. My anxiety became unbearable and without more cocaine my thoughts were turning to mass paranoia, coerced by days with no sleep and only alcohol for fuel.

A young Mexican guy walked by the window, again and again, looking in, *maybe to monitor my position?* It was time to make a dash for it. I collected my thoughts and decided to trick the authorities who were obviously about to bust me. My plan was to nonchalantly standup, then suddenly and with extreme speed, dash for the door, run across the street, and run as fast as I could for as long as I could. *I wouldn't look back.* I would simply sprint as fast as I could. *I am fast as shit.* If I found a ditch or a bush, I could jump in it and hide. *They would never find me.*

I stood up and pretended to stretch. Then, I turned and pounced for the door. My movement left me awkwardly jamming my arm into the glass door. Over my shoulder a person stood up and shouted something. I muttered something about being ok, and opened the door with the opposite hand.

I stepped on the street and went to run. Over my shoulder I heard, "Ashore! Help me."

I started running. *What the fuck was that?* Fuck me. I ran faster. My thoughts got the best of me and my planning went to shit. I slowed to a walk. Then a stop. Then I bowed my head and looked down for the longest time, panting. "Fuck." I expected a Federales to shove an AK in my back at any moment.

Nothing happened. I was outside and it was a beautiful sunny day. The crowded streets didn't notice me. *Was that Bluejay, back there? What was wrong with him?* I walked back to the corner and peeked around an adobe brick building. There was a man curled in a ball beside an entrance to a bank. Bluejay? I walked towards him, looking left, and right, and over my shoulder at least a dozen times before I made it across the street. It was Bluejay, shivering with his arms clutched around his knees. "Bluejay?"

"Dude, what the fuck? Where were you?" He yelled at me. His face was covered in tears, his eyes were swollen and shut.

"What happened to you bro?"

"They fucking pepper sprayed me."

This last sentence triggered something uncomfortable in me. "What about my $100?" Bluejay had gone off to find us more Cocaine. I was too paranoid to go with him so he told me to wait in the lobby of the closest building – I was sobering up.

"Who cares about your 100 bucks man, they fucking pepper sprayed me!"

I could see he was hurt, but I was really scared now of coming down. "Hey man. Are you ok. What can I do for you? Did you get robbed?"

"Dude, they fucking took me to an alley and held a gun to my head. They took everything. They took my fucking Coast Guard i.d. man. Fuck your money. Get me out of here."

As he was talking, I caught a reflection of myself in a window, and I almost laughed. A giant cowboy hat rested on my head, face covered in days of scruff. My wifebeater was covered in a brown stain. I looked down to analyze it and saw I was wearing sandals that weren't mine.

"Are you even listening to me? Ashore! Fuck man. Help me out of here."

How Bluejay found these guys, I don't know. But he got in the back of their pickup truck. They drove around the corner into a dark alley and robbed him at gun point. They pepper sprayed his ass. He stumbled back around the corner, across the street, on an adrenaline high, and became so disoriented that he just sat down on the street and curled into a little ball. He was literally ten feet from me as I sat in paranoid panic moments before. His current mood was anger. Mine was anxiety. I wanted coke and Bluejay wanted to be safe aboard the ship.

I helped him up and we slowly walked the best way we could – downhill always leads to the water – boats are on water. He kept his eyes closed so it was slow going. I just assumed we'd get arrested before we got back. Suddenly, and out of nowhere, a van pulled over beside us. The passenger door rolled open with a slam, and to everyone's surprise, Seaman Gabriel, Coolk, and a group of girls (who couldn't have been more than 16) were on the other side.

Coolk yelled, "Ahhhh, hahahaa, look at you crazy fucks!"

Then Gabriel, "What happened to you guys! Haha! Get in the van, bros. Jesus Christ."

YARN 16

GABRIEL, SEAMAN

Back in San Diego, I was eligible for a room and rack in the barracks. The chief in charge gave me first dibs at who'd I room with, and I quickly choose one of the new guys, Sheen, over the other option, Gabriel. In the chief's office I made some joke about getting roofied by the Jesus Lover. When I opened the door, the bastard was leaning on the other side and almost fell into me. Without missing a beat, he started:

"God Bless you."

"Dude, you need to stop with your holy roller shit around me."

"Well he blesses you anyways."

"I'm from the belt-buckle of the fucking bible-belt. So shut your fucking mouth when you're talking to me. You weird fuck."

"Jesus saves ashore."

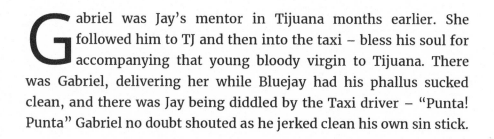

Gabriel was Jay's mentor in Tijuana months earlier. She followed him to TJ and then into the taxi – bless his soul for accompanying that young bloody virgin to Tijuana. There was Gabriel, delivering her while Bluejay had his phallus sucked clean, and there was Jay being diddled by the Taxi driver – "Punta! Punta" Gabriel no doubt shouted as he jerked clean his own sin stick.

Gabriel was the preacher aboard the Thrill. If he had alcohol in his system, he was a loud preacher. If he was fucking one of the new people aboard, they were most likely drugged or chloroformed, he was a sinner who needed Jesus. And if he anticipated hard work, he was the saint who had to volunteer his time with the Chapel.

Gabriel liked hermaphrodites and he was obsessed with his body. He posted photos of himself all over his locker. With a dark Thai tan, Gabriel was first generation American. His parents were both white missionaries from Thailand, which was the best joke of them all, that Gabriel never got! [Now that I reflect on it, maybe he was adopted. Woops.]

It was in each port-call that Gabriel would show up with a stupor and a lady-boy. He would shout at us, "Isn't she hot. Look at her. She gorgeous. A true child of Jesus."

We would notify him that the lady-boy had a penis bulge in her skirt, and he would look baffled.

"No. No! That's so gross guys. Haha Fuck you!"

YARN 17

GEORGIA, SA

"Who?" His Atlanta accent was thick and low. "Who?" He pronounced it like a baritone-child scrambling the letters and asking if he was saying the word right: "wHooooooww?" the inflection on the syllables were correct for forming a question, but a question wasn't needed. He knew who I was talking about. He just wanted to assert his personality.

"Her," I said. "Your girl's roommate... In yalls' bathroom."

"Wait. The tweeker bitch? You fucked that witch in our bathroom?"

"Yup. She asked me to help her shave her pussy. We got aftershave in our piss holes and sat in the shower for an hour afterwards trying to stop the burning."

"What the fuck Ashore! You're a nasty fucker."

"I snuck her into the barracks too. Took her tampon out with my teeth and threw it against the wall just above Sheen's bed. There's a big brown circle still there where it splattered on the wall. Don't know what happened to the tampon. You should look for it, next time you're there"

"Alright. Bro. Alright, stop. Don't tell me no more of that shit. Gross fucker... What-cha doing tonight? You can't crash here. My girl'd be pissed."

The first night after we returned from our deployment, a bunch of us went to an underage club near the Convention Center, and Georgia met some Palauan girl and went home with her. Within a week he started living in her apartment in Riverside, about 30 miles North of San Diego.

Driving home my eyes wouldn't separate, so the white dashes in the road merged together about 20 feet in front of my truck. I closed an eye. *Better.* It took about an hour to make it to Riverside and about 30 minutes to make it back to base. Given traffic. I was accustomed to the late drive, after dropping off Georgia. He would normally give me a beer to stay awake. The beer didn't matter towards the end of the week. I'd have to hang my head out of the window, to allow the rush of the 60mph winds to keep my eyelids open.

Normally, far in advance of arriving at the Navy Base gate, I would roll down my windows to rid the truck of smell and freshen up as much as possible. As I approached the gate, I'd pop gum, have a cigarette lit as entered. Each and every time a Navy MP would shine a light in my face and a second MP would shine a light over the things in my truck. Though the normal routine didn't apply one night. I had a full beer bottle in my lap as I approached the gate - I looked down, *Shit!*, and threw the bottle out the window – 100' from the gate. The sound of breaking glass was still in the air as I came to a stop and stared at the MP. He looked at me in silence for a long time.

"Aren't you going to show me your i.d."

"Oh shit. Sorry. It's been a long night." I gave him my I.D.

"Coast Guard huh?"

"Yeah, I'm a puddle pirate."

"You going to make it where you're going before you kill someone?"

"You bet. I got this."

"Get the fuck out of here. I don't want the paper work."

JOURNAL ENTRY

"Request permission to dispense with political correctness?" — USCG Captain Ernie Blanchard, 1996. (Mills, 2019)

(March 2003) Stagger asked if I was still interested in smoking Meth. I met him at Kurtz's place and bought my first bag. He looked at me and said "If you say a word to anyone, I'll kill you. I know where you sleep." He smiled as though he actually thought he could kill someone.

Tomorrow, Alaska. Series of three, always. This will be número dos. It will be good to get out of this shit hole. I'm fucking rotting away here. I need to get off this ship already.

YARN 18
NEDDLE-MYER, SA(S)

T wo last second new guys arrived at our ship as we left for our Alaskan deployment. We were at the explosive ordinance dock in San Diego and I had just been publicly shamed by the DCC for telling a group of longshoremen[49] our scheduled departure time. I was chain smoking to deal with my embarrassment and there came a white government van with two seaman-apprentices in dress blue[50]. *New Guys!*

After returning from Acapulco I made the rank of Seaman and was fully qualified underway, so Alaska was going to be good for me. Also, I had joined the Coast Guard from Anchorage Alaska and I was excited to be back in that part of the world. Having more new guys on the boat meant I was even further from the bottom.

We departed San Diego and putted north. Our first day at sea was accompanied by an all hands deck-force meeting. This was supervised by the 1Lt, Mr. B, and his flock of petty officers. There was the Boatswain's Mate Chief (BMC), the first class, two second classes, and about ten third classes. They all stood, with their arms crossed, some with dark sunglasses. We, the 30 deckies, sat on the non-skid decks. The two new guys in the center, unsuccessfully playing it cool. Mr. B. looked at a sheet of paper. All was quiet.

"What the fuck is this? I ordered one god damn non-rate. One! Neddlestogen? Meyerdick? Needle-Meyer, which one of you is Needle-Meyer?"

---

[49] Longshoreman: derived phonetically Along the Shore Man. A stevedore. A shoreside line handler.
[50] Dress-Blue: The formal uniform of the USCG.

The two new guys were being pointed at in a very crude way by each one of the warrant's hands (like they had a personality of their own (which they probably did)). They looked at each other and were openly confused, and worried.

"Not me, sir!" "Not, I," they said.

If my memory serves me, I think their separate names were Nedstrom and Meyerstrom, or something similar. Their barely congruent names were forced together by our savage leader, and those two unlucky bastards were doomed to be united as one man, for the rest of their days on the Thrill.

"Well, God Fucking Damnit," Mr. B. said with a smirk. "If you're not Needle-Meyer I guess I'm a son of a bitch. Am I the son of a bitch? Huh? Hey, Hey, haheha," Mr. B preached, looking around at the rest of us sitting in his presence. "Hey, Chief," now looking at the BMC, "What's the worst thing about a kid's birthday party?"

The Chief answered he didn't know and he left the boatswain hole in silent protest. All thirty of us maintained a blank face as we watched him go. He undogged the door, stepped through it, closed the door, and we all watched him latch each dog, one by one, in the correct pattern around the door. A tremendous silence followed the screech of the last dog. Needle-Meyers, both sitting in a stiff cross-legged attention, straight out of boot.

Mr. B. answered his own question, "Getting blood on your clown costume." More silence. "So. Gang, this is Needle-Meyer, Needle-Meyer, this is gang."

Before he dismissed us, he asked the BM1 to read out the mess-cook detail. "Ashore, Clark, Lois, Neddle-Meyer (one and two), Gabriel." Clark and Lois started whining and we disbanded to start prepping for rough seas in the Gulf of Alaska.

YARN 19

SHEEN, SA

The Thrill was steady as she went, north bound. I was back in the mess-cooking lineup, smoking to get on the outer decks. When we hit the 48th parallel the Captain secured the outer decks for rough seas, the smoking lamp[51] went with it (though there were ways to get around this). Through the Gulf of Alaska we slow-belled[52], for days. Sea sickness was a plague.

Stagger was facing him head on, in a quasi-karate stance. Without his dark-sunglasses, his Asian features came out. This time particularly, Stagger's squint was part of his presence. His white undershirt was already beginning to become transparent with sweat. Sheen's clothes were more drenched, you could see his shaved belly. His fat rolls were eating parts of his shirt. Stagger was moving his weight from one foot to the other. If we weren't in the tight space of the berthing area, he would have been dancing around the ring.

---

[51] Smoking Lamp: Before lighters, a burning lamp was kept in the galley for smokers to light their pipe with. It was inefficient and wasteful to use matches in heavy winds. 'Extinguishing the smoking lamp' is a phrase used to deny smokers the privilege to smoke. It could be used practically, when the ship is in heavy seas, the lamp was a fire hazard and being on deck would be dangerous. Or it can be judicially, to punish the crew for disobedience.

[52] Slow-Bell/Fast-Bell: an operational condition, or command, which expresses the speed of the engines and thus the speed of the ship.

There was no way Stagger could take down Sheen one-on-one. Sheen was too big for the guy. As Stagger bounced on his toes, Sheen stood flat foot and slowly walked forward. I was behind Sheen with the other guys, awaiting in exhilaration. Sheen was pissed. He always got pissed during these things. Stagger Lee was making jokes about his weight. Stuck in a corner was a pretty bad predicament for him. I was awaiting Stagger's cry for his gang, Legit and Ray, to come and pounce on Sheen. Sheen was waiting for it too. I was trying to decide if I would use fists or not – I was going to help Sheen when the others interfered.

Sneaky Stagger Lee, stuck in the corner, reached for the light switch and the room went dark. Instant noises of wrestling. Shouts of anger. People pushed passed me so fast I lost my stance and was too late to cover Sheen's back. I jumped on the pile of bodies on the deck and started swinging madly.

YARN 20
NEEDLE-MEYER, SA(S)

We had landed in Dutch Harbor, again, and this time I was not on duty. A month before we had hit the port and the entire island was frozen over. My duty that time was as the liberty-van driver and I spent 18 hours a day driving drunken sailors to and from, between bars and boat. Comfortable behind the wheel, and excited about life, my position as driver was perfect. If I ever had duty in port, I would want it to be as the driver. Though this port call left me free to do as I pleased. But in Dutch Harbor, with Cinderella liberty, there was not much to do under the age of 21. To the mountains I went.

With my new-found buddy Needle-Meyer, I walked off the ship wearing jeans, a t-shirt and hoodie, and my work boots, because they were water proof. The snow was about six inches deep and the air temp was somewhere in the 20s. The fueling dock is on the leeward side of the island, so the winds common in Dutch were unbeknownst to us, for a time. This is one of those picturesque memories I'll cherish for all times. Needle-Meyer and I were both under 21, and he had no friends onboard, so he naturally tagged along with me when he found that I was carrying a bottle of aristocrat vodka – fitting at that latitude, riding the international date line. And we climbed some mountain by our moorage, no path, just walked off the road and started climbing. The wind four miles later was tremendous and standing was nearly impossible, though that may have been due to drink and not just wind. My sailor bud was nervous and cold, we were both cold. I'm not sure what he did, but I remember him whining like a bitch because his feet hurt. He said he didn't think we were going to climb the whole way up, and I asked him to leave. He became quiet and kept following like a kicked dog. I drank.

The top of the mountain split in two geographical patterns; a slow long slope on the leeward side meandered down to the town of Dutch Harbor. Dutch is a fishing town that is a second home for nearly every fisherman who is headed to or coming from the Bering Sea. Its permanent inhabitants are a mix of Russian Americans and drifters. The other side; a 90° cliff that led 1000 plus vertical feet down into the crashing waves and ice below. The waves and wind on this side of the mountain had carved an almost perfect chair shape in the rock, overlooking the sea, 1000' feet high. It was my perch while the sailor kid whimpered and said "you're too close to the edge." I remember squeezing a chunk of basalt in one hand and a chunk of ice in the other, and the temperature made them feel of the same hardness. *King of the Basaltic Ice Chair high in the Aleutian Islands!*

Dutch Harbor, as well as many of the Aleutian Islands, is littered with a bunch of WWII bunkers. Many of the bunkers are in turn littered with broken glass and spray paint, an externality from a population being in other types of wars. Me and bitch sailor boy found one of these bunkers and added to the glass with my urine and a shattered aristocrat bottle. The view from the 50cal slot in the concrete was not as impressive as my God Chair on the cliff.

Back on the boat I was cornered by a BM and told I'd be covering a duty shift tomorrow. When I asked why, he said he could tell me that I smelled like booze but then that might turn into a Mast. I again was able to learn the roads and businesses as the liberty-van driver for my ship. There was something pleasing about driving a 15-passenger van around the island, through ice and mud, by dumpster diving Bald Eagles, after having dodged a mast for being drunk underage. Port towns are typically filled with sailors and fishermen trying to soak in the land in a matter of days, and Dutch Harbor is certainly no exception. Drunken fishermen, in season, in Alaska, and in the headlights of my van. Stumbling shipmates, slurring officers, and vomiting bosses racing to get it out, to get it all out.

D utch Harbor is well known in the sailing community (especially in the fishing community). It is the physical representation of the classic safe harbor in the harshest of environments. While it is mostly full of workers passing through, there just for a few days, Dutch has a very distinct culture that keeps its finer points throughout the passing crowds and external influences. The businesses and restaurants are inviting, despite the stereotypically intimidating drunk fisherman crowd. The locals appreciate the travelers and the travelers appreciate the locals.

I think most sailors like Dutch Harbor, or at least respect it. Many of my shipmates talk poorly of deployments north, and they mock Dutch. Though there is always subtle nostalgia when talking about Dutch with anyone who has spent significant time there. This makes me believe, and I do want to believe, that sailors like the romance of the island. Well, most sailors anyways. Needle–Meyer, well....

Needle–Meyer wasn't comfortable. One day I was called to the sick-room, which is the doctor's office on a ship, and there was Needle–Meyer. He looked loopy and the doc told me he was given a dose of morphine to coerce him to calm down. He said that Needle–Meyer had requested me specifically to accompany him before leaving the ship. Appears that he had told the BM1 that he was going to kill himself.

I was stuck on Needle-Meyer's hip, as duty, for the next 24 hours. Then, they flew him off the ship, after double dosing him with more drugs. And we never saw that Needle-Meyer again, though his double was still slothing around the ship somewhere.

YARN 21

JAY, SEAMAN APPRENTICE

We splashed anchor in the inlet of an island somewhere in the Aleutians. It was early spring, ice and cold were everywhere. Anchor-watch was new to me, though I learned quick and soon was given a break-in. It was Jay. She was having a hard time qualifying on anything and, during the time I knew her, never stood a qualified watch by herself. Our duty was to stand on the fo'c'sle for four hours, on the 0400 to 0800 watch, and report the condition of our anchor. We were wrapped in our parkas. I hadn't had sex in a long time. The Dirty Jay was a very real temptation for me in those hours, though it makes me gag now. I had a boner most of that watch, though it was nicely hidden beneath my parka, tucked hard against my belly, under my belt. My intentions are almost always honorable, and I would have had sex if the opportunity presented itself, though I was not interested in making the opportunity, it would have had to of been her. As she talked about her life story, I feigned an open ear, and I dreamt about pulling her pants down and cuming inside of her clenched cheeks. With hours to kill, a boat full of sleeping crew, and a minimally manned bridge watch, I could have pretended to show her how to take anchor readings, all the while fucking her, without anyone noticing, maybe, or maybe not. *So horny. Jesus.*

And she talked the whole time about being happy to not have to go to her church anymore. She didn't believe in god anyways. Her parents were mean to her and her sister, so they decided to leave as soon as they turned 18. She said her sister was smarter than her and that it was her idea to join the Marines, though they wouldn't put both of them in boot camp together, and she was scared to go by herself. They joined the Coast Guard instead. Boot camp was horrible for them and she always wanted to just give up, but her sister had pulled her through.

Does your sister like to fuck like you?

She gets a bad rap because she is friendly with everybody and boys take advantage of it. She doesn't like Alaska because its cold. She heard I was on the last patrol. She asked if I liked Panama.

"Oh yeah. Panama was good. We often had steel beach[53] and we all lounged on the fantail in our swimsuits. It was hot."

"I like the heat," Jay said, as the snow and wind blew around us.

"Yeah, the girls all wore skimpy bikinis," I said.

Jay blushed under her parka hood. I smiled and a major pulse of blood pumped under my belt.

The BM2 came out of nowhere. "You two are relieved to the bridge for lookout, send Legit down when you get up there. Don't fuck around up there. The QMC is in a shitty mood.

---

[53] Steel Beach: the outdoor area of a man-of-war designated for rest and relaxation.

YARN 22
KIDD, SEAMAN APPRENTICE

My head was kept down most of my first deployment, after meeting the Thrill in Acapulco. I was unsure how I was trying to develop myself given all the information that was unraveling before me. Boat life was exhilarating, and to this day, nearly twenty years after the Thrill, I find sea-life essential to my health. People, however, never have the same simulants to compel them. I was born a Virginian; my mother was an Appalachian. The sea was the polar opposite from home, it was an escape. The shipmates I encountered on the Thrill were from all different castes and domains. The people of California, too, sent a squall of culture to rock my core.

Kidd was from Colorado. Like many enlisted guys, he came from a conservative family. His goal was to provide for his wife and newborn twins – who were both born lacking skin pigment, they were albinos. Kidd was welcoming on my first deployment, and despite my stance to remain a quiet observer, he forced conversation and I soon considered him a friend. After the Acapulco deployment, while we were in home port, Kidd flew home to visit his wife and children. He came back a somber ship-wreck.

Kidd's wife was having a hard time raising twins, of course. And in the outdated Colorado town she lived in, the albino factor was too much. She was embarrassed to go out into town. She threatened to leave the kids and Kidd if he didn't move back home. The 1LT denied Kidd's request to terminate his enlistment early and offered no solutions. No strategies to overcome.

During the Alaskan patrol, Kidd and I hung out on the smoke deck every day after our work routine, to spin yarns over the railing. It's there that Kidd told me about his problems with his family and with the command. He didn't know what to do. We talked about his options and different methods of getting out of the terms-and-conditions of enlisting – not a good prospect. Claiming homosexuality was a solution he could use to get ousted, though it would be accompanied by mass hazing and possible legal repercussions for falsifying enlistment papers.

It was March, and we had anchored off of Nikolskoye, in Russian waters and ice. In an effort to promote international order, Coast Guard Headquarters tasked the Thrill to meet a Russian Ice Breaker to perform a dance of diplomacy. This set the crew in a position to slave to bring the boat off course by a few days, anchor, and standby as our captain had drinks with the Russians. Eventually our Captain refused the invitations to dine and drink, and he sent the DCC in his place - which was a great funny insult to the Russians. We lowered the Napoleon-like DCC in a small boat, which transported him to the Russian ship. Hours later the slurring Chief came back, stumbled about the deck, and in an admirably disorderly way shouted about Deck-Force allowing rust to build up on his ship.

That was to be our last mission on that deployment – getting our little Chief drunk with the Russians. Kidd was at his breaking point and was desperately concerned about his wife – there was no internet on board. Phone calls were limited to the one satellite phone on the boat; available during "non-sensitive" operational conditions, at a cost of $1 per minute, and limited to five minutes due to the high demand. Often crew would wait in line for an hour, only to have the phone connection suspended for unknown operational concerns. Kidd couldn't manage his anxiety in the waiting line, so he never called. Instead, he waited in his head.

Anchors were weighed and we were on the way home, where Kidd could discover the rest of his life. You could read the hope in his swagger.

We were transiting the Gulf of Alaska through 35' swells. It was the apex of my time on the Thrill. In the great North West aboard a ship blasting through freezing gales! Amped on coffee and rough seas, my excitement could have kept me sustained at sea for months. Apparently and unfortunately, I was the only one who felt this way.

It was 2003 and we had been underway for 70 days. The only two stops we had made were to replenish our dry stores and fuel in Dutch Harbor. We were all going home. Still wrapped in our parkas. Still scouring behind the seawhiz on the fantail to avoid salt water spray while we smoked. Randomly, a broadcast was piped[54] over the 1MC:

"NOW HERE THIS. AN ANNOUNCEMENT WILL BE MADE AT 1630 TO ALL HANDS. MAKE YOUR WAY TO YOUR QUARTERS OR MESS-DECK FOR A MESSAGE FROM THE CAPTAIN."

Instinctually, with static excitement in the air, we all huffed down our remaining smokes and bottlenecked through the doors of the main-deck. Huddling on the mess-deck, shaking off salt water,

---

[54] Piped: Historical a boatswain whistle would call commands to a ship's company. This whistle was also known as a boatswain pipe. Thus "piping" was the commands of the boatswain's whistle. The boatswain pipe is still used in the CG daily, mostly for customs and pomp, though the word "piping" is now being applied to any message communicated to the ship via the ship's 1MC.

there was a wet-dogs-covered-in-ashtray-resin smell. We stared at the speaker above the salad bar.

> *"Ladies and Gentlemen. Today is a day you will never forget. As per an executive order issued by our Commander and Chief, President George Walker Bush, the United States of America is at War with Iraq. As members of the United States Armed Forces, it is our responsibility to carry out the missions of the United Sates Coast Guard with the upmost devotion to duty. Your country has asked you to fight, and fight you will. I am giving the order to turn USCGC[55] WHEC[56] Thrill to course 350 degrees [we felt the ship take a sudden course adjustment]. Our orders are to protect the fuel depots located in the Southern portion of Alaska, the ports and harbors of Valdez, Cordova and Seward. We will [a background voice started shouting 'Right Hard Rudder!' − the 1MC went off.]"*

Our ship was suddenly slammed by a wave on our quarter[57] and a shudder sent everyone reaching for something to grab. Silence. A second wave made us widen our stances. We looked at each other. "Oh shit!" someone said pointing out the galley window. We were beam to the trough[58]. The ship rose like a cork, leaned 20 degrees to the port, and dropped 25 feet, rolled an opposite 40 degrees. Coffee covered the deck in seconds.

---

[55] USCGC: United States Coast Guard Cutter (Navy ships go by USS)

[56] WHEC: White High Endurance Cutter (aka 378)

[57] Quarter: In a relative position from the ship ranging from 90 degree to 180 degree, or 270 degrees to 180 degrees. Or the place on the vessel opposite the port/stbd bow.

[58] The vessel is parallel to the wave and the bow and stern will fall and rise at the same time.

The 1MC came on.

> *"Stand by for heavy seas as we come about."*

The mess-deck was silent other than some mess-cook shouting obscenities in the galley as dishes clacked and banged. I watched Kidd push through the crowd toward the foredeck, where Margaritaville was. We continued to get slammed on our beam[59] until we started hitting the seas at an awkward angle on our starboard bow, which created the most ridiculous rocking and yawing motion. We made it through and the bow started taking the seas dead on.

"Now hear this," the captain's voice was back on the 1MC.

> *"The Thrill has been charged with the protection of the petroleum ports in Southern Alaska. We will arrive at our destination in less than 24 hours. Carry on with your regular routine. All officers, warrants and E7 and above report to the wardroom."*

I found Kidd in his berth. Our objectives in the Coast Guard were not the same, and my reaction to the Captain's news was very different than that of Kidd's. Many of the crew became detached and silent the moments following the message. Kidd, I knew was beyond upset. When I saw him, he neglected to make eye contact and I left him alone. I wandered into the aft lounge.

---

[59] Beam: The side of a vessel, or at 90 degrees relative (270 degrees) to a vessel.

Later that evening the boat was in a standard routine. Less people than normal were in the lounges. I considered grabbing my guitar and heading for the boatswain hole but Kidd stopped me before I made it to my instrument. He whispered in my ear, "want to smoke some pot?"

We were behind the seawhiz – there are no cameras there and the wind would take any smoke out to sea, we were moving quickly. While each of us stood guard for the other, we made it through the better part of a joint. Instantaneously I felt a rush of paranoia darken my perceptions. Then another. I looked at Kidd, "Fuck I'm high. Dude... Dude I gotta go to my rack." I didn't wait for his response. I couldn't look him in the eye.

Quickly down the side of the ship on the swaying main deck. The seas were howling and delivering cold spray. I was drenched before I made it the 200 feet to the door I was looking for. *Please don't let anyone see me like this.*

I pulled up on the door's handle, and was preparing to surrender and confess if someone was on the other side. No one was there. Down the ladderway, transit the passageway, into Margaritaville. Ray, Stagger, BM3 watching TV on Jack Kurtz's rack. I didn't wait for them to say anything. Quickly I climbed into my rack and pulled the curtains closed. *Please don't open the curtains. Oh my God I can't talk. What if they open the curtains? What did I do...* For hours I laid in my rack, perfectly still. Afraid to breathe because I didn't want anyone to hear me, *they might want to talk.*

When the mind-set abated, I was left feeling depressed and worried. I snuck out of my rack, and sucked water from the faucet in the head. I quickly got back in my rack. *Fuck.* Sleep.

The next day I passed Kidd in the hall with our BMC. They had a bunch of paperwork. Kidd looked at me and smiled. He was happy. The rumors didn't take long to make it around the ship, they never do. Kidd, I was told, had smoked pot and then turned himself in. He did this because he wanted to be kicked out so he could move back home with his wife. *I wonder if I'll get to attend his mast.*

YARN 23

CLARK, SEAMAN

I t was in the early 19th century that Richard Dana took a leave-of-absence from Harvard and signed the documents needed to join a fur trading ship bound for California. Dana, being born a wealthy elite in New England, and being extremely well educated, was obviously not the prime candidate for this position, or surely the captain and mates must have thought so, though he had pull in high places, and maritime companies needed sailors. So, off Dana went, two years before the mast, to work as a blue-collar sailor and eventually to write about his experience.

C lark was a smart ass mother fucker. Too smart. He was not well protected, like Dana was. He lacked influence with his superiors, and he lacked a legal team back on shore. Clark was by far the smartest guy aboard the Thrill. He also, and I don't believe it to be coincidental either, was the most reclusive drunk aboard the ship. The miserable bastard and I would stand lookout watch together. As my trainee, he quickly learned the simple functions of the watch and we then used our time talking astronomy. The Thrill was not only an ocean-going ship, she would also run dark, and the combination of the two would place her flybridge as the finest spot on the surface of the Earth to stargaze. There we would ponder the utter useless existence we are all bound to. Clark was a great shipmate to talk about pain and suffering with. He was a truly miserable man. I've always wondered why salt heals some?

Journal Entry: I think Clark is suicidal. It's like he thinks he's smarter than everyone and it's driving him nuts. I think he's smarter than everyone too. Mr. B. is making his life hell. Haha.

While underway, like a stowaway, Clark was not to be seen. If sought, he may be found chasing rust or painting, though he would do these tasks in isolation, unwilling to converse. On watch he would do the minimum. On shore, he would stand his duty and return to the barracks. Clark would open up to me under the correct conditions and explain that he was better than everyone else, that our shipmates were all idiots, and that alcohol seemed to be the only escape from the chaos of being a non-rate in the Coast Guard – I agreed with these things. Despite my admiration for this pitiable squat fellow, we never fraternized beyond his never-ending miserable stories. I would watch him flounder around the base, trying to overcome his drunk to make it home, or make it out somewhere.

It was the first week back from Alaska that Clark started "missing movement." This was a term used for being late for a watch or for a duty rotation, even when the vessel was moored fast. His excuses held no weight with the command. One day Clark reported late, and came up with the excuse that he thought it was a different day. I believe he mistook a Wednesday for a Saturday. After a mandatory alcohol and drug test, Clark was sent to a rehab clinic without further word. I spoke with Clark once after that, and he said that Rehab was ten times better than the ship.

Clark was the second non-rate I knew to go to rehab in the first year aboard the Thrill.

H is Captain's mast was in the wardroom. It was one of many I'd go to, though I went to that one on order from the BM1. In full dress uniform, twenty of us non-rates lined the bulkheads of the wardroom. The tables had all been moved out, and seats were aligned as if the place were a courtroom. There was an uncomfortable feeling where my spine connects to my head, a pulsating pressure. I felt horrible for Clark. Clark entered and ineptly marched to the center stage, BM3 JJ following behind as his Petty Officer representative. "Captain on Deck!" a voice shouted. Everyone stood at attention. Clark was swaying like a spinning top, just not spinning. "Be seated," the Captain said.

The ship's yeoman read a list of charges against Clark: "Missing movement; Absent Without Leave; Count two of Absent Without Leave; Drunk and Disorderly; Consumption of Alcohol on Duty;

Disregard for Duty; Abandoning Post...." I listened in disbelief. This was my first mast. There was lots to learn.

The Captain responded: "Seaman Clark. How do you plead?"

The "Captain's Mast" has a long history. In the glory days of the Royal Navy, ships were all sailing vessels and the Captain would hold all-hands quarters in front of the mast, where there was minimal deck gear. The Captain would stand on an elevated platform by the mast for his announcements. These meetings also included non-judicial punishment proceedings, whereby the Captain would act as judge and jury, following the law despite his abilities. Before the turn of the 20th century, punishments typically included floggings. Seaman found guilty of anything would be sentenced to receive X number of lashes by the Captain's Daughter[60]. The perpetrator would be bent over the Gunner's Daughter (a cannon which sits about 3 feet off the deck) and lashed to the deck by each limb. The whipping would commence. After the torture, the seamen would often be left to suffer tremendous pains from exposed nerves, infection, and blood loss. As vessels switched to steam, coal, and finally gas/diesel the iconic mast changed form, but the name stuck.

BM3 JJ was responding for the trepid Clark. "Seaman Clark pleads not guilty, Sir."

"Not guilty. I see. Petty Officer Garcia [YN1], can you read me Clark's service record please."

YN1: "Seaman Clark has one negative page seven for not completing his helm/lookout watch qualification in a timely manner. Clark has one negative page seven for not completing his in-port

[60] The Captain's Daughter is another name for the Cat-o'-9-Tails, which is the same thing as an 18" whip used as a justice device for misbehaving sailors. The whip is traditionally stowed in a bag, hung beside the captain's cabin. If you and your shipmates don't want to get in trouble for a misdeed you've done (say sodomy) then you'd say to each other "don't let the cat out of the bag."

watch-stander qualification in a timely fashion, with a punishment of Port/Starboard rotation for an undisclosed amount of time. Seaman Clark completed basic training on February the 1st of this year and arrived to The Thrill on March 1st. Seaman..."

"I've heard enough. Clark? I want to hear it from you. Do you have anything to say for yourself?"

Trembling Clark spit out a few formal courtesies and started breaking up with emotion. "Sirrrr. Capton Sssrrr. Yes Sirrr. I belibe Imm not guilty sir. My intentions were..."

The Captain interrupted again. "I don't think anyone here cares about your intentions Seaman Recruit Clark. We are a well-oiled machine, each dependent on the other to function. You let your shipmates down. You slowed down The Thrill. You've abused us. Now. Given the testimony here today and your own words and your lack of evidence or witness, to prove the case against you is void, I leave it to your shipmates to speak on your behalf. Is there anyone in this room that will come to Clark's defense?"

We all waited for BM3 to do his part, to stand at Clark's defense. He never did.

"Then I find you guilty of the following charges. Missing...."

His voice faded from my mind. I honed in on Clark and could see his tears, even though he was looking the other way. His eyes no doubt closed behind his dork glasses. His fists were tight by his side. *Should I have spoken up for him?* Why didn't someone else speak up for him?

"Clark. You are hereby an E-1, to be labeled as a 'Seaman Recruit' until you're off this ship and well clear of this base. You are suspended to this ship until you are processed out. You are suspended without pay, indefinitely. You will be leaving the United States Coast Guard under conditions 'other than honorable.' Now get out of my sight. Dismissed."

The BM3 had to call an order because Clark was too stunned to move. "About Face!" Clark turned remotely. "March." And off the pair went down the center of the wardroom, through the forward door that leads to the main deck. The Captain stood and someone shouted "attention on deck."

"Dismissed."

YARN 24

GEORGIA, SN

Palauan chick was mad at him. Something about not being around enough, too many deployments, work hours, blah, blah, blah. Georgia said he didn't want to spend his few months home hearing her bitch, so he started hanging out with the barracks' gang more. First stop, Tijuana.

We had just scored an 8 ball and I was trying to convince a hooker to touch my nuts for one dollar. Neither Georgia or I were into hookers, but a brothel is a good place to find drugs. The 8-ball disappeared at some point and we must have looked like crack heads trying to find it in the disgusting hooker-party bar. We were scouring through the couches, retracing our steps to the bathroom and generally panicking. I found the missing 8 ball in my pocket minutes earlier, though I wanted to play it off like I hadn't for some reason. I was high and my thoughts were by no means clear.

"Georgia," I said with my head hung like a puppy. "I have it man."

"What! You found it?"

"No, I've had it this whole time."

"What the fuck. You fucker!"

We proceeded to the nearest bathroom. "Whhhhewwwww!" "God Damn!!!!!!!"

Out on the street with escalated heart rates, we felt good. My jaw massaged itself, and a small dopamine surge inched its way up my spinal cord. Neither one of us was thrilled about being in Tijuana so we started to move back to the boarder on foot. Some guy came up close to us and asked for a cigarette – he seemed like a homeless guy. My sweaty palms reached in my pocket to find a smoke for the guy.

Blue and red lights flashed on a passing car, which then quickly slammed on its breaks and pulled onto the curb directly adjacent to us. Two figures popped out and started running to us, yelling something in Spanish. "Oh fuck." I heard Georgia say.

"No te muevas! No te Muevas!" They had drawn their side arms and I saw Georgia and the homeless guy backing up to the building we were beside – a brick building covered in graffiti, a single lamp draping over the side walk illuminated the scene, with blue and red lights shooting through my brain, *the bricks looked beautiful,* the homeless guy against the wall with all his limbs spread, "ready to be searched," I thought.

Georgia looking at me with a panicked look "Ashore. Ashore. Move fucker. Get against the wall. What the fuck. Ashore." *His accent is so fucking funny.* The cop in my face and screaming. He was pushing me and I could feel his steel club on the inside of my thigh, rubbing aggressively. It felt good.

A drip in the back of my throat sent a dopamine hit to my brain that was unbearable – "Oh God Damn," I said loudly. Then in a whisper towards Georgia, "that's good!!!"

Georgia looked at me in disbelief – "Oh god, fuck me."

The cops were screaming. I was back to the wall at this point, staring at a pulsating flashlight. They held my chin up with that steel club again. *Do I have powder in my nose?* They did the same to Georgia. Then I saw them frisking the homeless guy, in front of us, to display the deed neatly. They pulled out a baggie of white powder from the homeless guy's pocket. "They just set us up," Georgia said over my shoulder. A cuff went over my wrist. The other side went over Georgia's wrist, and we were hustled into the back of the car with blue lights. "Fuck." "Fuck." How many times was the word "Fuck" said I don't know. The opposite door opened and the homeless guy was flung in beside us. The car started moving.

My body was so enraged with energy. I needed to squeeze something. Jump. Run. Yell. Fight. *Fight? Fight? Fight or Flight?* The positive sensation in my veins pulsed fierce. I looked at Georgia and I knew his experience was not like mine. I was exhilarated. *So fucking full of throbbing energy!* "You poor bastard," I thought as I stared at him. Georgia looked at me, again in disbelief, "What's wrong with you?" He said.

"We're good man. WE. ARE. GOOOOOOOOD." Is what my mouth spoke. "We can get out of this." *Did I say that out loud?* There were two cops in the front seat, who were smaller than us. The homeless guy beside us is probably a third cop in disguise, but I saw his hand-cuffs, so he is out of the equation. *Maybe if we use our cuffed arms to choke out the driver.*

"I can't go to jail, I have duty tomorrow," I whispered to Georgia. He wouldn't even look at me. I pulled his arm up with the cuffs and motioned my plan as best as I could. Whispering, "let's choke him!"

Georgia just blurted it out. "How much? Amigos, how much money to let us go?"

The cops were looking back and forth. "10,000 pesos" one of them said in perfect English, "Each."

"That's $500," Georgia said frantically.

"Ok, ok. The ATM gives $300 American. You give us $300 American and we let you go." Georgia looked at me.

"I don't have that kind of money," I said nonchalantly.

"Ok, OK, $300," Georgia said.

The car did a U-turn, and a prospect hit my head. I was about to be alone with these guys, Georgia walking back to freedom without me. In jail. No communications. A young white kid. *Mexican prison.* Kicked out of the Coast Guard. Framed. Locked up. Abused. Dead. "Oh god, Georgia you gotta help me."

"Ashore, I can't get that money out man. Even if I had it, it won't let me take it out."

The car stopped. The door beside me opened. They un-hand-cuffed us and sent me to the ATM. I had $45 and could only withdraw $40. "That's all I have, sir. Please."

They pushed me back. Yelled something. And put me back in the car. I watched Georgia, from the deadly silent backseat of the cop car. They had a baton to his back as he typed away at the ATM. A lot of talking. Georgia was crying. More typing. Again, more typing. They were at the ATM for minutes? Something was wrong. The cop came over, opened my door, ripped me out of the car and threw me to the ground. A boot on my chest as his partner took the hand-cuffs off. "You get fuck out of here. If I catch before you make border, I take you to jail!"

His foot released pressure and I scrambled to stand. Looking around I saw Georgia in the distance scouring down the sidewalk across the way. I chased after him. "Georgie. Georgia. Georgia!" When I made it to his side, he wouldn't look at me. "Which way to the boarder?"

"I don't fucking know. I don't fucking know." He was shaking.

"Fuck man. Fuck. This is fucked." We were all alone on a dark street. There was no one. No street signs. Just adobe buildings everywhere. We crossed an intersection and could see a glow in the distance and we adjusted our route. "I'm fucked up man. Seriously, what are we snorting?"

"Stay the fuck away from me Ashore. You're a fucking lunatic. What the fuck is wrong with you." I didn't know what to say. I hadn't processed the night yet. *Was it my fault?* I started ruminating in my head. We walked faster. He wouldn't talk to me.

A neon sign was in the distance and I convinced Georgia to go in with me to ask for directions. "I have a few pesos man. I'll buy you a drink." We went inside. A laser stripper show. This wasn't tourist Tijuana. These were all Mexicans, in a dim and relatively quiet bar. No one was cheering. No one was talking loudly. No one was soliciting. Georgia tried to leave but I grabbed his arm. "I'll get us a beer and get directions and then we'll go." I was feeling better. My freedom had spiked relief deep inside me and my endorphins were running again. "O la seenior. Dose servaceas poor four vour?" We sat on a couch together about 15 feet from the stage. I sank into the cushion with a Modelo in my hand. *Cold.* Cool sweat from the beer on my palm.

Sinking deeper into the soft couch cushions. My heart beating hard. The early symptoms of a dopamine rush creeping up my neck. *Deeper into the couch.* Cold beer on my lips, ran down my chin a little. A brown girl on the stage. Wearing high-hip panties and nothing else. *Moving slowly.* Her eyes closed. Long black hair. Gracefully sliding her naked curves to a beat. *Slowly.* Her rhythm was like liquid euphoria. *She's high.* Her body glowed in the laser show lights, which seemed to move almost backwards they moved so slow. A little sweat on her skin on her hip. More sweat on her shoulder. Her body couldn't have applied more elegance to the movements she felt. A pole allowed her to defy gravity. My heart throbbed and pushed a beat all over my body, in my brain. Sparkling ecstasy behind my eyes. My stomach let out a smile, like a car going too fast over a hilltop. Lasers flashing colors and traveling around, probing things. She watched her arms, which leisurely followed the unhurried lasers across the universe. My mind was experiencing the same euphoria that the stripper felt. *Was she a sex slave? Not much more than a teenager. Can it be wrong to feel so good?* I felt so very good. A green laser travelled across her breast as she arched far back on the pole. Her glossy black hair fell with flow in slow motion to the deck and she opened her eyes for the first time. She was looking at me. *She saw me.* She saw into me. And I into her. We were twins in dreamland rapture.

Georgia said he couldn't believe I forgot how much he spent. I honestly didn't remember him telling me. I knew something went wrong at the ATM, but other than that I didn't know. Our beers finished. We bee-lined it to the border silently, aware of things behind us. We made our mess-cooking duty at 0445. Despite Georgia's negative feelings towards me, we hid in dry-stores while he slept and I stood watch over things and ate M&Ms.

YARN 25

DOZER, SN

J ack London wrote, "Show me a man with a tattoo and I'll show you a man with an interesting past." The ink aboard the Thrill was mediocre. Some of the older guys were covered with it, some of the newer guys would rush to tattoo parlors in foreign ports to catch up. One beautiful seaman on our boat, I forget her name, had a back piece that would give a Chihuahua a rager. Dozer was one of the few younger guys who was covered head to foot – he must have had a waiver to get into boot.

He was big and jovial. Hairy and loud. Friendly and talkative. When I arrived, Dozer was the "paint-locker" guy. This meant that his duty was to manage the paint locker and distribute the correct paint to whoever needed it. It also left him in charge of the Hazmat locker. My interactions with him were minimal throughout the day, though often enough on the smoke deck. His tattoos were mostly traditional: a heart with "mom," symbolizing his mother was dead; a Hulu girl symbolizing he'd been to Hawaii and knocked up a local; a swallow on his shoulder, symbolizing he'd traveled 10,000 miles at sea; a transvestite Jesus on the cross. All these tattoos were barely visible beneath a thick mat of fur.

I had served five mess-cooking rotations when Dozer was due to transfer. He had struck the rate of BM and was due to transfer to a ship out East. Before he left, he was tasked to pick a replacement and train them on the duties of the "paint-locker guy." Dozer spoke with me about this and I was in a position to coerce him into picking me. The BM1 approved my appointment and within a day of shadowing Dozer I had transferred into the locker.

spent my last few months on the Thrill as the paint-locker guy. I kept the locker tidy as shit, though I was ultimately pretty lazy at it. Once I decided to huff a can of "green-death," which was a horrible smelling part-A engine bilge epoxy. A little nervous and wanting to prevent detection, I closed the paint locker door and secured it shut with a line from the dogging assist handle to the firemain. In the true bow of the ship, a room with no ventilation, which is a fire safety feature, not a personnel safety feature, I was locked in from the inside with a giant open can of green-death in front of my face. I put a plastic bag over my head and placed it around the open can. Huff one. Huff Two...

I sat back in a rocking chair and looked down at myself peeing. I was in my childhood pyjamas and the Captain was on the way to inspect the ship, his next stop was the paint locker. So scared. I was covered with pee and I couldn't stop rocking the chair. My chest was hanging out and my dick looked like a massacred vagina. Oh no! Please no, don't let the captain catch me like this. There was a banging on the door. He can't open it. "Get up," I yelled at myself. "Get up." A banging again, this time closer. I was running upstairs. I was sprinting up the stairs. Running. The banging got louder. BANG BANG BANG. It was inside my head. BANG! BANG! BANG!

I jumped up, through sweltering perspiration. I looked around. I was in a paint locker. The door was tied shut. "What the fuck," I mumbled and raced to the door, untied it, and swung it open. No one was there. Nothing except a blast of the coldest fresh air I've ever felt. I was in my uniform, no pee. *It was a dream.* I looked back and the can of green death sat open on the deck.

YARN 26
SEAMAN RECRUIT SHITFACE

I don't know if anyone remembered his real name. I don't remember anyone's name from boot camp. Hate to jump from the Thrill to basic training, but it relates: I'm about to include a letter from Neddle-Meyer's mother.

Within a week of Basic it was obvious that Seaman Recruit Shitface had mental deficiencies. His face was slightly cock-eyed, like that character in Forest Gump. He always struggled to get words out and he always failed to reply as mandated. A simple "Sir, yes Sir," was all that was needed in most situations, and Shitface couldn't do it:

"Yes, ssss, ssss, Sirrr. Sir."

"What the fuck did you say to me!?!?!" the Company Commander[61] would yell back, pecking the bill of his ranger-hat against Shitface's head. "You stupid fuck! You can't say it can you? Say it! Say 'sir, yes sir' Now shitface NOW!!!"

"Eye, I, Petty Offff......"

"God Damnit Shitface, I said say 'sir yes sir!'"

"SSSSsssss, SSSSSssss, SSSSSiiiiiiir, Sir Sir."

And the routine would continue in a similar fashion for days...

White t-shirt hanging out of the uniform – Shitface. Unshaven face – Shitface. Off step in formation – Shitface. Has to go "peepee," – Shitface. This guy couldn't get it right. The company commanders made a plan to have him give up, to kick him out, to make him leave in pain, to quit. One of them brought in a music CD with a carnival track on it, the one you may hear as the clown car passes by at the

---

[61] Company Commander: the USCG version of the classic Drill Sargent.

Barnum & Bailey Circus – "doo-doo-doobee-doobee-doo-doo-dooooo-ooo." And they would play that track in the dorms when they wanted to summon Shitface. And they would summon him a few times a day. If we had a second to breathe, to shine our boots, or reef-tuck our racks, we would all find a moment to sigh and relax. Then the clown-car-song would play. We were all required to chant "Seaman Recruit Shitface, Seaman Recruit Shitface,....." As the song played, "doo-doo-doobee-doobee-doo-doo-dooooo-ooo," and Shitface would scurry down the center isle in his best imitation at a march. You could then hear the barrage of yells commence through the office door.

He was gone one morning before reveille. His rack was made, his gear gone. He had flunked out and sent home for ever. A week later, an unknown Lieutenant came to our barracks and mustered us. At attention, he walked up and down the center aisle, and a man presented as a Doctor from the CG Jag Office tailed close by. The Lieutenant reminded us that we had sworn to fight for our country. That the United States was under attack, starting with the great tragedy of 9/11. That, as soldiers, in the United States Military we had to protect God and Country, and we were obligated to protect the United States. He said he was sorry to pass on information regarding our shipmate so-and-so [Shitface], that he had passed away a day earlier. The Jag officer then proceeded to warn us about confidentiality, classified materials, and judicial punishment procedures for dealing with violators. He said that the Coast Guard's legal team was doing everything it could to help Shitface's family. In addition, the CG reserved the right to monitor all incoming and outgoing mail, and it would be monitored from then forward, so please do not seal envelopes.
"Carry On."

YARN 27

NEEDLE-MEYER, GONE

Copies of this letter did not survive, nor did they get distributed to the rightful owners. I did not receive a copy of this letter, and thus must forward it by memory. Fuck me for not knowing his actual name. I'll just use his boat name – It makes the letter less depressing anyway...

> *Dear Deck-force Team,*
>
> *It is with great sorrow that I have to inform you of the death of my son, your shipmate, Needlemeyer. Needle-Meyer ended his life on June 5th of this year. He is remembered by me and his father and younger sister. He will be buried at the Baptist Church in Flag Staff Arizona on the 10th of this month.*
>
> *Needle-Meyer had nothing but great things to say about his time on the Thrill and the adventures he had at sea. He specifically remembered his kind shipmates: Chief Marks, Seaman Ashore, and Seaman Sheen. You are all invited to his memorial service on the 10th.*
>
> *Fair Winds and Following Seas*
> *Needle-Meyer's Mother.*
> *November 8, 2003*

Mr. B. said we were welcome to go to sick-call "if we wanted to cry about anything." The BM1 moved through the water tight door. We all watched him. One dog at a time. Open. Step through. Close. All dogs shut, except the one with no gasket, left swinging.

A moment of silence...

"Seriously. If you want to cry about anything. Sick-call is open for the next five minutes."

YARN 28
KATHERINE, SEAMEN APPRENTICE

Katherine Whatever-the-fuck-her-last-name-was, was my fuck buddy from the boat. An awkward relationship I cannot seem to burn from my memory.

Techniques to deal with hazardous materials on the Thrill were minimal. Double bagging was the standard effort to prevent spills and cross contamination. Between paint and solvents, most bags turned to a sticky vapor-dense mush on the bottom of the hazmat locker. To clean the mess up, the BM1 gave me all of Deck-Force on our first in-port work day after the Alaskan deployment. With my first assignment in a leadership role, my busy mind was finally focused.

The Monday arrived and I was given permission to skip the morning muster to prep the HazMat chain. My method was simple: Form a line with 20 deckies down the length of the main deck, pass the triple sealed HazMat bags over the ship to a second line on the quaywall. That second line would then deposit the HazMat in an awaiting bin the Navy provided us for the purpose. As the paint locker guy, and the lead of the operation, I was in the HazMat locker ensuring each bag contained only items that could be submitted together: i.e. oily rags in one bag, solvents in another, etc. The locker was below the second deck, just aft of the paint locker. Its only access point was a small hatch and a 15 foot ladder. I began the process at the bottom of the ladder passing triple sealed bags up. Suited up in a HazMat suit and full-face respirator, I felt isolated from everyone, though they all knew their simple tasks.

Everything was going smoothly. The BM1 mentioned that he didn't like how we were passing bags over the water, but he didn't offer a solution so I ignored his unease. The bags went from triple bagged, to quadrupled bag out of concern of leaks. I was nearing the bottom of the HazMat pile, scrapping goo off of the deck, when a voice yelled down from the hatch above. I looked up and saw Lois and another female face.

"Hey Ashore! We have a new deckie. Katherine, meet Ashore. Ashore, Katherine."

She was a brunette, with long hair. Not wearing an undershirt under her working coveralls, I could make out her entire collar bone and a few inches of her chest, though the outfit was too baggy to see her breast size. I gawked upwards in silence. She smiled and said: "Hey Ashore. Maybe I'll get to see your face in the barracks tonight." And the two disappeared.

In my full-face mask and respirator, I was invisible to her. *Lois's going to tell her I'm a drunk. Oh shit! Barracks tonight? Oh man, I bet she invited her to the barracks!"* My focus switched to tactical mode. How could I land this cute new girl? I sucked at meeting women. Planning on how to get Katherine in bed with me became my core thought. Bags still going up the ladder. Goo scraping. Fucking Katherine in my brain.

The night came on and I was chugging whiskey. Bluejay said she was hot, but I still hadn't seen her in full. Tired of being alone. Tired of masturbating. Tired of the fucking boat. Everyone else getting laid. It was my turn. More shots. Swigs straight from the bottle. Lois and her friend never stopped by. *I'll go to her door.* I put a condom in my teeth, and knocked on Lois's door. No answer. *Fuck.* Walked back to my door. It was locked. *Fuck.* Where is Bluejay. *Fuck.* Sat in the hallway. Another swig. Hallway swaying.

I could hear the elevator door open around the corner at the end of the hallway. I looked down at the tiles beneath me and considered my ability to stand – it wasn't looking good. I looked back down the hall. Lois and Katherine had stopped and were looking at me. They started laughing. *Here's my chance.*

Always nervous when we hung out, I drank to calm myself. When we had sex I couldn't cum. On the boat I would half brag about my success to the guys, and half worry that the command would find out. *My head was a mess.* When the Thrill left for another Southern patrol, we were considered a couple by most of the crew, though for me the whole thing was awkward. I didn't really know her, and there was no way she could have known me. Without the comforting effects of alcohol, I tried to ignore her as best I could.

On the fantail, deckies would sit in circles, or lean on the rails, smoking and joking. I'd walk off on my own, stare off into the distance and she would come stand beside me. Breathe in my ear, "hey sexy, you think we could crawl into the line locker tonight?"

Suck on my cigarette. "Maybe."

YARN 28

Journal Entry: (February 2004)
Sometimes I can hear, the loneliness of the sea.
When I'm wrapped in her arms, and she whispers to
me.

In Manta she lied to me. Said she forgot her i.d. in San Diego, so the command wouldn't let her leave the boat. When I returned later that night, it was rumored she'd left with the OS1. I didn't complain or blame when she fucked him. The guys used it as a reason to give me shit. I blocked the assaults by saying I was bored by her. Katherine and I would still talk as if nothing changed. She was confused by me.

YARN 29

GILMOUR, SN

Nineteen-Seventy: drugs had America's attention, thanks to the American political pulpit. With monetary considerations and influence from the church, specific presidential and congressional politicians pushed anti-drug policies. Before being impeached for abuse of power, Nixon had become a devotee of Billy Graham and declared a "War On Drugs." The War On Drugs was established and prioritized within the Coast Guard's core missions. The Thrill was built for it – by Billy Graham and the evangelical movement.

The War of Drugs leaves a tremendous trail of death. This trail starts at the doors of the cartels in Central and South America. The power these cartels have is derived by the illegality of cocaine in the United States. Among the innocent people that are killed by the War on Drugs are the drug runners and their families. For the drug runners, go-fast coxswains in our case, they are only mules. US Courts have found that 70% of these individuals are forced into their roles by cartel violence. Their families are often held hostage until the drugs are delivered successfully. They are told that, if they complete their mission their family will survive. If not, their female family members will be sold in the sex trade and the males will be suspended from the ceilings by their testicles. The assignments given to the mules are always to transport drugs on a specific vessel to a specific location in the United States, stopping at refueling ships disguised as fishing vessels along the way. These captives are given a side arm with one round and set off on their mission.

Our job on the Thrill was to prevent these people from making it to the USA. When we succeed, we take their drugs and pose in front of American news cameras with the American Flag waving over our shoulders. We then load the drugs into giant white vans and we go to the local bar and drink until we decide to scrounge the streets for drugs.

On my third voyage south, our gas turbines had major engine issues and we were forced into a nearby port – Puerto Quetzal. There, with pigs and little children on the street covered with flies, a group of seamen, including Gilmour and myself, headed for a five-star hotel. A robin-egg blue pool waited empty in the center of the mission style complex, shaded by giant palms. We paid $20 per room, and as a compliment were allowed to watch the room-attendants skip around in short-skirts and tank tops. The front desk sold Jack and Modelo, which listed formaldehyde in the ingredients. The Reds they sold supposedly used fiberglass in the filters. I purchased as many of each item as I could carry.

One morning I found myself hanging onto the side of the pool, submerged, in my jeans, pissing myself. Exhausted, I couldn't make my arms pull my body out of the water. Looking up at one of the room balconies, I saw the FSC and QMC laughing with two young room attendants. Both chiefs were married, I knew, and I sat there staring at the balconies in intrigue. Fat bleached pig skin hung out of their wife-beaters. They laughed. Drunk on the euphoria of the moment. Nearing ten in the morning, I had been in the pool since before the sun came up. My Jack bottle was full of chlorinated water which I sipped to diffuse my dehydration.

Gilmour walked by me casually. "Hey fucker. Help!" He startled, laughed, and coached me towards the stairwell where I could crawl out. He lit a cigarette and pressed it against my lips. We laughed at the shit hole city we were in. We laughed at our attitudes towards it. We discussed the probable quality of the cocaine there in the nearby town. We supposed it could be found easily by flashing money around. Soon we were *on the road.*

S waggering down the streets, we searched for a low-key environment to chat with the locals and fill our stomachs. The town had evidently heard that a bunch of white people had arrived, and a restaurant owner threw out his cigarette and smiled as we approached. He hustled us into his building without us understanding a word of what he said. Food was brought out without us ordering. When you're underway for long periods of time, your equilibrium becomes compromised, I started swaying. Gilmour ordered me tequila to help my hurting head.

We ate fried shrimp (head, shell and tail), with a fantastic layer of powdered spices. There was a young girl of about 12, in a clean white dress, helping us nervously. I asked her if she knew where we could get cocaine. "Coca? Cooooockaaa?" and I placed my finger to my nose and sniffed. "WHEWW!" I shouted way to loud and smiled. She ran into the back room.

A frantic man, who was probably her father, came flying through the door. "Senior. Help you, senior?" he said.

I repeated my Spanish word for cocaine, "Coka? El Coca?"

"Oh. Si amigo... uh... Quieres Cocca?"

"Si," I said, hoping he had understood me, and he retreated to the backroom. The tequila had boosted my confidence. Gilmour was occupied, feeding the roosters and pigs on the front stoop of the restaurant. They were arguing over the scraps. The girl from earlier was peeking through the kitchen's doorway curtains, also watching the animals eat, with contempt.

The meal was small, and the drink was enough to make us not care. Encouraging us to go outside, the owner introduced us to a man wearing a cowboy hat on the street. We threw a random amount of loose change on the table. "Grace-e-us Amigo."

We left the restaurant and soon found ourselves riding in a rusted 1960s German minivan. The city streets were dirt, though they still gave order and a sense of civilization amongst the buildings. Soon we were on backcountry roads, in the jungle, flying through dusty country sides, past little huts and men on horses.

There was no stereo for the faint plastic country music to exist. But there it was, in a ceiling corner of my brain, softly twanging away. Gilmour was arched in his seat. Eyes on the window. Watching for our unknown destination. Senses on alert. I had my own alertness to deal with. The past 24 hours had been a mixture of adrenaline, excitement and euphoria. It was fading, and there was no replacement in sight, not even a source of clean water.

The country music was torture so I said the first thing to pop to my mind: "Why is our ship white?"

He jerked his neck, to bring his eyes towards me, and he scanned my posture and face. "I don't know, why?"

"I thought we were supposed to be sneaky. White isn't sneaky."

He turned away again. Our van was moving up and up on a dirty mountain passage. Continuous cowboys and rusted trucks passing our windows. A rickety school bus nearly plowed us off the road. Present beneath a layer of red dust, a hint of lush jungle. The city was a long way behind us. We both had bad thoughts in our head. And the driver wouldn't respond to our English.

As we moved on, I could see my shipmate's stress grow. It was possible we were being kidnapped. Maybe we would be taken to a jail, a fucking cage in the jungle. Both of us played it cool, silently. There was nothing for us to do. *What could be done? Jump out of the van? Fucking driver won't answer our fucking questions. How far would the walk back be? We could deny asking for drugs. Deny, deny, deny. Our Coast Guard careers would be over. Locked in Guatemalan prison. Gilmour would be assaulted first I bet. Look at him... I'm just a flabby little bitch. Nobody would rape me.*

Without warning the driver swerved. For a split second I could see Gilmour's head smash against the window, then I was on the floor. Spanish filled the air in loud three-round bursts. Working myself to my knees I looked out the windshield. We had skidded off the side of the road and came to a dramatic stop. A small overlook exposed the pacified sea in the far distance. The driver flung open his door and stomped to the front of the van.

Gilmour and I looked at each other without talking and we hopped out of the vehicle. We lit cigarettes and watched our Mexican driver fiddle-fuck under the hood. He came over and gestured for us to shut the door, and rubbed his fingers over the van to show dust was getting in. He then casually walked back to the hood and slammed it closed. He jumped in the driver's seat, and slammed that door too. We stood speechless as he peeled onto the street, towards the way we came. Leaving us like we were assholes, or something, covered in fine red dust.

"Fuck."

YARN 30

BLUEJAY, SN

H e had laundry duty as I had paint locker duty. Underway we were both isolated in the front of the ship, while others were doing other menial work. Of course, both of us had helm/lookout watch too, and were even on the same shifts. 4 to 8s[62]. Because of the early hours we would have had "late-sleepers," which allowed us to sleep until 1000. Because we had special assignments, laundry and paint locker, we could not sleep in and we had a line of people bitching at us as we raced from our bridge duty to our special duty. Amongst this schedule we continually had to be ready to respond to daily drills, at random times, and daily mass hazing activities. Bluejay and I became very close during this time. Seafaring is a struggle, plus you are always mad from a lack of sleep. I loved it.

Once Gilmour came to "get some paint" from me and we found our way to the laundry area. There was Bluejay, listening to "Friend of the Devil," with the largest smile on his face. I've never seen anyone look so free as I did see Bluejay that day.

"She says she's got my child, but it don't look like me. Set out running, but I take my time. A friend of the Devil is a friend of mine." (Dead)

---

[62] 4 to 8s: Watch at 0400 to 0800 and a second watch at 1600 to 2000, every day.

Gilmour and I both were ten years junior to Bluejay, and we were influenced by the guy. His ability to enjoy music so shamelessly. *Sans souci attitude, towards everything.* After seeing Bluejay like that, Gilmour and I often found reasons to visit him during the work day. We talked about everything. We dreamed about getting off the ship. Traveling to Europe together, where Bluejay had $10K hidden in the mountains of Switzerland. Bluejay often spoke about his drugged adventures in Philadelphia and his escape from that scene just in the nick-of-time, when he joined the Coast Guard. "They would have killed me, I owed them so much money."

On our 4 to 8s we were in a position to see the orange sun rise and the purple sun set, every day, from the flybridge. There, at the highest deck of the ship, was isolation. It was a fantastic spot to dream, think, and stare off into the distance. The job was easy – report everything. A brass sound tube was at hand, to talk to the bridge below. A giant mast decorated with spinning electronics, lights and flags. A walkway around it with a place to take shelter from the wind and smoke, against standing orders. There was a pair of big-eyes, a telescope, to spy on the moon.

The sun was still up, I was riding high. We were in the second hour of our watch. I leaned on the railing by the big-eyes, staring at the fo'c'sle. My mind ruminated in a peculiar way, and I let it. Sea spray was coughing through the anchor hawsers[63], and water was racing over the deck, flooding off through the scuppers. The paint on the deck gear; yellow, red, rust, shinning brighter. The anchor chains

---

[63] Hawser: a hole cut through the deck of a ship to allow anchor chain to freely fall into the sea.

disappeared off the ship. Two giant bitts, a windless, chain, chalks, a bulwark. *Paint so reflective.* My senses honed in and I started mildly hallucinating. It wasn't my first LSD flashback. The deck gear suddenly looked like legos. The quality of an object is a result of the merit of the stare. Water shooting through the hawser pipe turned into Legos. I was hesitant to look at my hands, but when I did, I thankfully found them in reality.

The sound tube's[64] buzzer squealed, signaling the bridge wanted me to communicate. I opened the brass sound tube and said, "flybridge."

Bluejay answered, "The OOD wants you to come down."

---

[64] Sound Tube: A copper pipe designed as a fool proof and primitive way to talk between decks. A bell horn on either side, both to speak into and to amplify sound. A electric buzzer normally nearby to attract awareness.

YARN 31

QMC

Wasn't supposed to be drunk. There was a Cinderella liberty. It was 2345 – fifteen minutes before we were to be locked aboard, most of us were getting in a last second piece of land. There was a group of us talking about rock and roll. Who was the best? I was heated, emotions never being my strong suit. The QMC was definite that the Rolling Stones were the best, and he was articulating why. I couldn't take it and I started shouting about why he was wrong. Not sure what I was saying, though my shipmates around me were trying to get me to calm down. I had lost all sense of respect, hierarchy, and order. At the top of my lungs, "no one is better than The Mother Fucking Boss, man! No One!" I was dragged down the gangway by someone. My feet were picked up. Tossed in the shower. Cold water soaked through my shoes. Felt the sway. Slurs and commands.

I awoke the next day, vaguely recalling the incident, and worrying about what would happen when I showed my face. No one ever mentioned a thing. I don't even like Springsteen that much.

YARN 32
MS. MILTON, ENSIGN

During the early years of the 21st century, like many government organizations, the Coast Guard was doing everything it could to diversify its ranks. This meant they recruited lots of women. And because women are smarter than men, they were mostly officers. Ms. Milton was one of these women. She was about 5' tall and had skin too tan to be white. She wore C sized breast and a beautiful face.

During southern patrols, the Captain often opened the decks to "steel-beach." This was a clever term used to describe the fantail during sea-going liberty. If you were not actively on watch, you could use the fantail as if it were a beach. Crew would bring out guitars and lounge chairs. The Jacob's ladder[65] was lowered so we could swim. A shark-watch[66] was posted. A legitimately good time was had by most.

Ms. Milton and the other female officers would come out in the smallest bikinis possible and flaunt their bodies to each and every shipmate. Small and tantalizing. Glistening with sun, lotion and sweat. Sexy in their suits. Sexy in their stances. Sexy laying down. Delicate on the nonskid.

Turnover. Can't get comfortable. Try to relax on the knees, yoga pose, with head down and butt up. Still not comfortable. Walk to the railing, lean over, look at the water for a bit. Widen stance, lean over farther. Put feet together, reach up on tip-toes, bend over. Think

---

[65] Jacob's Ladder: a ladder built of manila line and wood steps, designed to stow in a bundle and easily drape over the ship for boarding. Often used in personnel recover or pilot boarding.

[66] Shark Watch: an armed watch stander prepared to warn of, deter, and, if needed, shoot at potentially aggressive sharks.

about getting in. Laugh out loud with a giggle; giving away the fact that you know everyone is staring at you. Turn around and exclaim that "hehe, I would jump from way up here if I didn't think my bathing suit would come off. Hehe." Stretch on your tippy toes again, stretch out arms, complete exposure of smooth stomach and under boob, pretend yawn.

M asturbating was a tough skill to acquire aboard, though it was necessary. There were three good options. The first was to do it in the shitter stall, in the head – the backside of the stall door was coated in years of congealed and hardened seamen spray. The second was to do it in your rack – which was more comfortable, though you risked being loud and then being caught. The third was the shower. I mastered the third, and I would rip out a page of a porno magazine and stick it to the wall in the shower. On this day, with my memory, I did not need to rip out a page while I showered. I also later noticed the back door of the stall was oozing more than normal.

If someone was suspected of masturbating in the shower, you would scream at the top of your lungs, "did you remember to wear your shower socks!" Then you'd punch as hard as you could through the shower curtain.

CAPTAIN

> *"Now hear this. Ladies and Gentlemen. Your country is indebted to you. It takes bravery and commitment, strength, to do what you do. At 2400 hours last night I gave the order to make all speed home. We're going home!"*

YARN 33

SHEEN, SN

We shared living quarters[67], everywhere. Voluntarily. Slept within penis reach of each other, for two years. Sheen's anger spells appear easily in my memory-recall, though his voice, his manners, his ideology is vacant from my recollection. *I know we were close.*

Images of his car in the dessert. His girlfriend Hannah – a boat chick. Mess cooking. We planted raw eggs in the hard-boiled egg bin. Waited for some unsuspecting sap to crack one open. The boat heels over unsuspectedly. Laugh as we hear deep-sink dishes crash to the floor. The FS3 shouts bloody murder. Clark curses god, and darts towards the doors through the galley. Balancing a pot of oil in one hand, as he quickly opens each dog around the door. His concoction doesn't make it over the side. It's on the deck flooding the alcove. FS3s and Clark yelling and looking for help. Sheen and I hiding in the scullery laughing in a fog of steam. Racing through the deserts of Southern California at 70mph, in his brand-new silver convertible Eclipse. "Go faster!" "I don't want to get a ticket." He was embarrassed about his weight. They found out and laid it on thick. Sheen dieting. Exercising. Running. Perspiring. Made friends with the Captain during morning runs. He's losing weight. Grinding his jaw. He's eating dieting pills. Weight loss pills. Bluejay and I take them for fun. Awake for days. Disgusted by pills. "Sheen you gotta stop taking these, their like speed. You're going to have a heart attack." "Shut the fuck up." He wears his skin like a cheap Wal-Mart suit. He plays plastic country on his dvd/cd player,

---

[67] Living Quarters: To quarter is to split into 1/4ths, to separate. Living quarters is then an area separated from working areas. (This applies to "giving quarter" as well: to give room or a room.)

Tim McGraw, as I drift to sleep. He leaves for work and doesn't bother waking me up, we have the same shift.

In our berthing area, Sheen bunked directly beside me, with only a thin sheet of porous metal between us. We were both on the top rack of 3-highs, located in Margaritaville. 3-highs are built with three individual racks stacked on each other, and each rack has a horizontal locker, roughly 5 inches deep under the mattress. When a locker is in the opened position it is called "tricing[68] your locker." If a person happened to be in his rack while the locker was opened, it was called being "triced." This was considered a fun way to haze, as it left the person completely trapped, and unable to see the person(s) who victimized him. Sheen was a big boy, so it took two to trice him. Sheen was never one for aggressive play and any attempt to fuck with him led to anger, which a lot of us thought was funny.

At one point, maybe in Alaska, Sheen was triced at the same time as me. We both rolled into the inboard side of our racks and were smashed there against the thin metal partition. We were smushed against it from either side. Sheen was irate. He yelled at the top of his lungs. The berthing area petty officer, BM3 Kurtz, came over and saw Sheen triced. "You better shut the fuck up or I'll give you something to whine about."

Sheen snapped back, "You better let me the fuck out of here."

The BM3 had been on the ship for three plus years: "I'll tell you when you can get out of there. If you don't shut your fucking

---

[68] Tricing: To move a rack to its vertical position, either as a daily cleanliness and order mandate or (when available) to use the locker beneath. To trice a person is to trap them in their rack, to haze.

bitching, I'm going to hand cuff your ass to the fucking fire main and tape your mouth shut."

I was right in the thick of it, behind Sheen and behind the partition, the BM3 didn't know I was triced too. I was worried Sheen was about to say something stupid. "Chill out, dude. They'll let us out."

"Fuck you Ashore, don't fucking tell me what to do."

He fucking yelled at me. I was trying to help him and he yelled at me. "Kurtz. You want him to shut up? Let me out of here and I'll make him shut up."

The BM3 came over to my side laughing – "I didn't even see you in here. Who the fuck did this to you? Haha." He let me out.

I walked over to Sheen's rack and he was breathing heavy. Angry caged beast. I was mad at his remark and determined to get revenge. "Can I have your cuffs?" I looked at Kurtz. All of the mates in the berthing area were peeking out of their racks to watch, and others had come in for the show at the sound of Sheen yelling.

"Ashore if you fucking touch me, I'll kill you."

"Let him go."

BM3, Legit and Ray all pushed the rack up, with all their might, and then counted "One. Two. Three!"

The rack fell open and everyone dived out of the way. I jumped under Sheen as he flew out of his rack in his tighty-whitie underwear. Not anticipating my move, to submit to being under him, Sheen had his back to me. I reached around under his arms and grabbed his neck, to let him know I was serious. When he stretched his primary arm backwards to grab my arm pit, I put all of my body over his left side and forced his fat arm up, twisting, and then took it back down towards the bottom rack. The cuffs were dangling by my belt. I had just finished Boarding Team Member Training[69] a week

---

[69] Boarding Team Member: an entry level Maritime Law Enforcement Qualification.

earlier and was quick with cuffs. I had the cuffs on his wrist and on the bottom bunk's hand-rail in seconds. He had my jaw and was trying to rip it off my face. I kneed him in the groin, did a summersault over his head, crashing into the bulkhead and I pushed myself off with the full force of my legs. I was back on top of the wild-boar, who was trying to figure out his cuffed situation. Pouncing for the other arm I yelled "someone get the tape!"

Ray came running, ready, with duct-tape he kept for such purposes, and he jumped on Sheen's head. Kicks were going everywhere.

Legit was pissed his rack was being used for the chaos. "You better stop kicking my shit boy," and he jumped on top of Sheen's lower body. Ray got the tape around his face a few times. He fucked it up and wrapped up his nostril too, but Sheen wouldn't stop fighting so we had no time to fix it. Next, I pinned his arm against his body so we could duct tape that too. In the period of a few minutes, Sheen went safely from his rack to duct-taped, hand-cuffed, and asphyxiated - covered in sweat and pink skin. He was still kicking in his tighty-whities as we all dismounted him.

"Stop kicking and we'll let you breathe," said BM2 Kurtz. Seeing the dangerous of staying by the drama, people started clearing out.

"Sheen," I said, "stop fucking kicking, jackass, and I'll let you go. Asshole." I was soaked in sweat too, but I was in my uniform with boots on. My watch was in ten minutes and the BM3 and I had to go.

Bluejay walked in the berthing area. "Hey dude, what's going on. I heard you were in a fight." He didn't see Sheen.

"Naw man, I'm good." I looked at Ray. "Hey brother. I've got watch. Can you take care of him so I can go smoke?"

On the fantail I lit up with Bluejay. "You look like shit, you can't go to the bridge like that."

"It's dark. No one will see." My cigarette butt was soaked in finger sweat so I ripped it off, threw it overboard. Inhaled hard on the filterless smoke. Kept the tobacco-stick between my teeth to prevent it from spoiling. Blew it overboard.

"You worried about Sheen?"

I started hacking my lungs out as I responded: "Maybe. He's a bigger bitch each day he's on those pills. Dangerously hormonal."

MR. B.

"Hey! Hey Ashore. Hehehe. What's the best thing about a nine-year-old. Eh. Ashore? Hehe. What's the best thing about a nine-year-old?... If you put her in the shower and slick her hair back, she looks like she's six!"

JOURNAL ENTRY

(April 2004) In the darkness of the berthing room, the edge where the head door meets the bulkhead illuminates enough for us to make way. Now, that door isn't shut properly. A crack large enough to cast a light beam exists and it has landed on Kurtz's rack. His curtain is slightly ajar. The boat sways. Perspiration on his forehead catches the beam of light. He stares forward, at something on the other side of the curtain I cannot see what. A whisper screamed at the far side of the berth. Kurtz turned instinctually. He caught my gaze. He looked at me, not my eyes, not my face, he looked at my head. Stared. Time left as I watched him staring at my head. Stiff face. Look at me! He pulled the curtain all the way closed.

YARN 34
SEAMAN ASHORE

There was nothing worse than watching the boarding team leave the Thrill at sea. The helo was different, working on the helo seemed improbable for someone like me. The small boat however, was manned by guys my age or just slightly older. *I could be on the boat.* Exciting operations. Risky and adventurous. Over the horizon. When GQ2 was called and we manned the gravity davit, my heart always sank. I wanted to be on that small boat so bad.

There were many reasons for launching the small boat. The primary one was to chase go-fast drug runners. Our small boat was a newer model, designed to go faster in larger seas, and further, over the horizon. It was equipped with two 250 horse power outboards. The coxswain would sit in the center console, a small windshield in front of him. Horse-style seating ran fore and aft for the crew, holding like hell to a leather strap. When the call was made to launch, our response time was supposed to be within minutes. The Boarding Team would arm themselves and prep while being debriefed by the Operations Officer. The boat crew would prep the boat, strategize for the number of crew that would be on board, and gear-up depending on sea conditions (swell size, water temp, time of day). Deck-force would man the small-boat launch deck with all hands. Each launch required a davit-man, and rear linesman, a forward linesman (me), a painter handler, and a winch operator. The order of operations had to be precise, to ensure the boat made the water without capsizing instantaneously and to ensure the crews weren't thrown off by the pitching and rolling of the Thrill. Of course, there were a bunch of white-hats (officers/chiefs) standing around directing.

Once the small boat was launched it would immediately come up to speed and start moving away from the Thrill, and disappear to some fantastical place. It was this that always left me feeling empty. It was horrible to know that something, somewhere, someone, was having a more exciting adventure than me. Back on the Thrill there was just a lot of standing-by to standby. Horrible waiting.

Once having served my time as a non-rate, I was allowed to enroll in an "A" school[70]. Georgia and I had mutually decided to sign on to the Airmen Mechanic "A" school together, which was a six-month waiting period, followed by a six-month school. I was on the Thrill longer and was permitted to enroll first. Georgia submitted our paperwork as I went to stand watch. The satisfaction of having a discharge date, of leaving the Thrill was tremendous! Knowing that I was going to work on helicopters, that one job that was so unreachable months before, was soothing.

As the months went by Georgia and I continued to go through the stages of being a non-rate on a 378. More paint locker adventures. More Mexican nights. Many more trips to Riverside. Our deployment which would have led us through the Panama Canal failed when our gas turbines blew up. We moored in Puerto Quetzal for two weeks instead.

---

[70] "A" School: The USCG has two standard classifications of schools: "A" and "C" schools. "A" schools are prolonged school where an serviceman learns his rate/trade which he will have for the remainder of his career.

Werner were half way through our home-port break when the day came. Twenty-five percent of deck-force reported to work expecting to receive orders. To have papers in-hand to leave the Thrill, and to venture into either new permanent stations or to "A" schools. As always, we mustered in the Boatswain-hole. Stagger standing on the side in dark glasses and pressed uniform. Legit beside him, leaning on the wall like he was driving a gangster's Cadillac. Sheen, on the far side of the circle, sitting cross legged, day dreaming. Gilmour, chatting with Bluejay, neither on the list to get orders. Lois, talking loudly and looking around for attention. Jay, scratching her crotch. Mr. B. walked in the room and the BM2 yelled "attention on deck!" Everyone jumped to their feet except those of us who saw the gawky old man enter.

"Yeah, yeah, yeah. Hey Now. Fuck you. Sit the fuck down everyone. Sit the fuck down. You fuckers are excited," he started his spiel before we were ready. He just dove into it. "But I need to get this damned ship painted in the next two weeks. Everyone shut up. Ray?"

"Yes, sir."

"You still don't have orders. I'm fucking stuck with you another six fucking months. Stagger?"

"Hey, sir."

"What are you striking or something. Ok. Ok. Hehe. Hey, Stagger. What were you doing over by the ball park? I saw you over there." Stagger stood still and gave a silent stare through his dark sunglasses, annoyed he was being interrogated by Mr. B. He started to respond, but was too slow. "You dangling your wee-wee through the fence? Hehe. He. Heh. Dangling your johnson through the fence at the playground?... Shut up. Hehe. Georgia?"

"Here." The boat rocked against the pier.

"Georgia. You're going to Elizabeth City. You're going to be an Airdale[71]. Congratulations. I didn't know you were smart enough for something like that. Bemberton?"

"Aye."

"You're going to Petaluma. Something about computer school. Davil, you are going to Petaluma too, to be a cook, we'll get you up to the kitchen to start learning, now. Hey Boats," pointing to the BM1, "get Davil up to the galley by the end of the week."

"Will do, sir."

"Johnson? Johnson you fucking traitor. You're going to Yorktown to be a Damage Control guy. Let's get Johnson hazed real good before we kick him to the engine room, hehe... Rhyile? [Rhyile was congratulating Georgia and not paying attention.] Where the fuck is Rhyile?"

"Rhyile Aye, sir."

"Oh fucking swell, thanks for wasting my fucking time. I should have you fucking flogged for this shit. What is it, 0900 already or what? Are we going to paint this fucking boat? Rhyile, you're gonna go to BM "A" school next month, start fucking packing, you'll miss this upcoming deployment... Needle-dick. Needle-Meyer?" There was silence, but Needle-Meyer number two was sitting in front of me. "Needle-Meyer, how the fuck did you get orders so fucking fast. It says here you're going to SK[72] school. I guess your gonna miss me. You want to work with the SKs before you leave, huh? Well you can't. Gotta paint this boat. Haha. Ashore, what's wrong with you? You hung over? Heha. Been drinking with Clark again, eh? Been playing the rusty trombone with Clark, eh? Eh Ashore. A little rusty trombone? Alright. Get to work! Boats has the floor."

---

[71] Airdale: a Coast Guard member who specializes in flight operations.

[72] SK: Store Keeper. The stigma is that Store Keepers are the shit bags of the CG. They choose the rate because it is easy, often landside, and advancement happens fast. It Is also a quick way to get off the ship.

I was exasperated. *Where the fuck are my orders?* Denial kicked in, *he must have skipped me.* Once the BM1 finished we broke to start the day. I was in the paint locker so I had to deal out a shit ton of paint. Fuck me. I did that and by lunch time I was at the Chiefs Mess asking for the BMC. "Hey Chief, what's up with my orders? They didn't come through?" He listened to my story; that I was ahead of Georgia on the list by one spot, and that it was assured I'd have orders. He saw my sense of desperation and must have been in a good mood. He took me to his office and we jumped online.

"See, no orders. But the good news is, you're first on the list for the next class. You'll have your orders six months from now."

B ack in the barracks, Georgia was kicking it with Sheen. I had refused to give him a ride to Riverside because my truck needed an oil change. I lied horribly back then. My anger had risen to an uncontrollable level and I was drinking to stop thinking. People were talking about the orders that everyone received. Who was leaving the boat in the next few weeks. Who was transferring out of deck-force. "We must be getting a lot of new guys, because everyone is leaving," some fuck said. I just sat there drinking. Georgia, Sheen and Gilmour approached me. Gilmour said, "oh you'll be alright man, just six more months." Then Georgia, "yeah stop being a little bitch, you'll be..." I swung at him before he could finish his sentence. I missed because I was drunk and probably didn't really want to hit him. The group jumped on me.

"What the fuck Ashore?"

YARN 35

LOIS, SEAMAN

Mayra yelled and ran to catch up. It was Friday, 1300. Bluejay and I were walking across the foot bridge that connects the shoreside to the waterside, 32nd Street Naval Base. Our plan? Buy a 30 pack of booze and drink it as fast as possible.

"Would you guys slow down please? Geeze... What'cha up to this weekend? I am going to the beach. I bought a new bathing suit. Hehehe."

It wasn't so much that we disliked her. As a shipmate, there was a tender place in our emotional seascape for Lois. We were just annoyed by her. Each style of smile she wore showed signs of plastic. Each comment she made was worthy of game trivia. Any flowing conversation could be halted, redirected, or smashed, without a loss.

The day was young. Through the barrack's small dirty window one could look out, across a mighty field of Naval supply ships, patrol boats and amphibious warships, beyond the Coronado Bridge, past Aircraft Carriers, and out further than the Point Loma Lighthouse, into an afar glittering sea of expansive horizons to sail to, forever.

All four of us sat crookedly in the little cinderblock barracks room. Two sandwiched on Bluejay's love seat. Me and Gilmour on Sheen's bed. Sheen, on the road in a car heading north alone, for the weekend, sober. But we were twelve beers deep, already searching for change to buy more.

"Alright gentlemen. I have a lady that desperately wants my tongue. You boys stay out of trouble." Gilmour left to enjoy his new fling with some girl that had reported to the Thrill earlier that month.

"Boys are so gross."

Bluejay turned up the music and pulled out three beers. "Drinking game. Finish the beer before 'Black Throated Wind is over." He pushed play on the dvd/cd player.

I pounded the beer in my hand before grabbing the beer he was handing me. I looked out towards the Point Loma Lighthouse, and was quietly disappointed I could never see its light.

It was near 1700 and our small party was dying. We had consumed our 30 cans, built a pyramid, and were working on the second 30 pack. Random mates came and went. Obscene things were yelled. Strange fluids pooled in the hallways and on the carpet. We were all walking with the legs of seamen. Lois was now talking about sex. "It's not that I'm waiting for marriage."

"Lois. It's not so serious. It's just about feeling good. Being open. Connection. Fun. And if your saving your virginity, maybe we could just have anal?"

"Yeah, Lois. My dick's not that big. It wouldn't hurt."

"Anything in the butt hurts."

"I have logs the size of coke cans slip out of my ass. A little glow-stick sized dick could go unnoticed."

Bluejay coincidentally had a glowstick in his pocket. He had jacked it from training earlier that day. "Hey," he said with a jovial voice as he pulled out his possession and waved it in the air, "what if we actually shove a glowstick in your ass, Lois? You think your butt would glow?"

The conversation faded from my conscious. Time vanished and I transported: I was outside, in a fog of piss beer, smoking with FS3 Carramat. "Dude. I scored some ice from Stagger. You wanna get high?"

I slurred my way through a "no" and explained my fear of being cracked out all weekend. But as I talked, he dipped his fingernail into a bag, pulled it out and held it to my nose. I sniffed.

Bluejay was gone. *Did I piss him off? Does he know I'm high? Oh shit, what if Sheen comes home. I'll pretend I'm asleep. Shit. Is it still Friday? Did I miss Saturday?* I laid in bed and covered myself. The sheets felt good. I knew I could pretend to be asleep if anyone came in. My jaw was grinding my skull. A lot of time went by. Ruminating on horribly dull scenarios, each scaring me deeper into my sheets.

I managed to put a porn dvd on Sheen's TV. I wasn't horny but I needed to distract my painful thoughts. My eyes locked into the screen and my head stiffened like it was locked into a medieval pillory. Two and a half hours I stared, then pushed the play button to watch it again. My dick ended up in my hand. I had to push play again. And again. Lotion was everywhere. On my balls, stomach, the dry-rotting carpet. Dehydrated. The more I jerked off the more my high increased. I didn't feel cracked out anymore. I wasn't paranoid. I was flying. Beat it harder, and harder. The volume of the porn was shaking the desk speakers. *On my knees naked.* Leaned back. "Oh God!"

An orgasmic explosion shot through my sphincter, my spine, my neck, the back of my eyes. I tumbled to the stale carpet and spasmed. Jerking, as if I were having a seizure. I laid panting. Couldn't believe what had happened. The movie continued playing and I just laid there in a pull of lotion and ejaculate – muscles twitching. Euphoria rushing through my body and brain. Largest orgasm I've ever had (to this day).

M onday rumors said Lois had been gang banged by Stagger Lee and BM3 Kurtz. She seemed happy about it.

YARN 36

SEAMAN WILLIAM

"Ashore, why don't you paddle. I'll paint?"

"Yeah sure, that's cool." *I'm going to have a fucking heart attack.*

William was more or less quiet, and we rarely talked, and worked together even less. I heard stories that he was dating one of the girls on the boat, and they had a secret rack somewhere on the boat (I could never find it). Our task was to paint the boot-stripe[73] around the Thrill, at least the part of it above the water line. Using a little row skiff, we set out to do this at 0630. I was decongesting from a three-day bender, and hadn't slept that entire time. My jaw was moving on its own accord, and the sweat pouring off my skin had already soaked through multiple layers of clothing.

"You alright bud?"

Oh my god no. What the fuck am I doing. I couldn't catch my breath as I pushed the oars through the water. All I had to do was keep the skiff close enough for William to paint the boat. "Sorry man. Rough night."

He put his roller down. Looked up, to make sure there was no one watching us. Lit a cigarette and grabbed an oar. "Why don't you take a breather bud. You look like you're going to die on me."

My hand was visibly shaking as I went to light my smoke. William looked away, down at the ripples between our skiff and the Thrill.

---

[73] Boot-stripe: an area of a boat painted with copper-based paint which rubs off easily if algae grows on it, always by the water line.

YARN 37

FIREMAN LEONARD

H is newest contraption looked like a piece to a paint ball gun. The one I purchased weeks later was aluminum, and could be held comfortably, without freezing your hand, while the nitrogen dispersed. Leonard's new toy was a whippet holder. A little steel cylinder that allowed the user to huff small eight-gram bottles of nitrogen without using a balloon. His device, and later the collection of all of our devices, was only the beginning to our huffing experiments in the barracks. Nitrogen is to this day enjoyable, though Leonard didn't think it was enough. He brought Keyboard cleaner: "wawawawawawawawawawawaw." Then he brought freon, "this stuff can freeze your lungs." "I get second dibs." Sickness, like waking up to a never ending Robotusin trip underway. Unsure if the sway is you or the boat. Headache. Stomach burns. Crawling to the head. Possible diarrhea, too scared to test it. Extreme nausea. Spinning. Darkness.

Leonard's type of desire, to get high on anything, was common for my shipmates on the Thrill. Seems that it's common for the Coast Guard in general (maybe for people in general). We compared stories of boot camp and surprisingly both found that we had used a similar tacit to experience conscious change there.

SHIPMATES

BASIC TRAINING: CAPE MAY, NEW JERSEY:

The Mexican Mafia was a group of three Mexicans from Delta company. They were talking about different ways to get high. One of them suggested a procedure which distorted sensory input to the brain. After a brief explanation, and much skepticism, I had to try. First, I bent over at a 90-degree angle to the floor, took 10 major breaths. Next was to rotate counter clockwise as fast as possible, while staring at a spot on the deck. Then, quickly stand upright, cross arms over your chest, and have a shipmate wrap his arms around your body, lean far back and pick you off the floor.

Blackness. Moving to the top of a roller coaster. Wind and screams howling by. Shit. Urine. Urine. Convulsing... Awake to a circle of people standing around, looking down.

"You OK man?"

"Shit. Did I piss myself? Did we get caught?"

JOURNAL ENTRY

(June 2004) Did you notice how Melville killed off every last one of his shipmates. None of them survived. And it was Ishmael alone that was risen from the casket, after the Captain found his leviathan. I am questioning my sanity. Haha. What the fuck am I doing in this fucking barracks! Aaaggghhh! Bluejay and I are spending too much time together. We gotta find somewhere to go. An escape.

YARN 38

CLARK

He didn't have a fucking home. I didn't have a fucking home. Shit, even Lois didn't have a home. "Home?" Returning "home" means going back to the Navy Base. Home is the ship. A pro-longed port call. *What is this Home? What do we do there?*

Clark was kicked out with terms "other than honorable" on his papers. He'd been awaiting his discharge as an E-1, mess-cooking, for months. He looked like a spider-ghost whenever I spotted him in the smoking area. He always walked off before I could say hi.

There was a moment, of less than an hour, he was given to clear out his shit from the barracks. Escorted by the Chief, a group of us paid respects by saluting him with raised beers in plastic cups. Someone yelled "good riddance," as the Chief and Clark waited in line for the elevator, "you over weight fuck." He was going home apparently. I was going to miss him.

MR. B.

"*I don't know why we bother with this shit. What? Ashore, you've been here for two years? You were trying to siphon milk from your mom's tit when I first got here. Two years aint shit. Is it Stagger? Well I guess we're glad you're leaving. What have you been fucking doing for two years. I never fucking see you. You hanging out at the playground Ashore? He eh? Huh? Hanging out at the playground with that uni-brow of yours or what?*

Well fuck. BM1 did all this work. He's the only one that works around here. Here guys, listen up. Ashore gets a recommendation letter and Thrill plaque from the BM1. Let's get this over with.

Alright. Alright. Get back to fucking work people. Ashore, get the fuck outa here."

YARN 39

SHEEN, SN

We had been close friends for over a year and a half. Completely different people with different viewpoints, different software running. We bunked beside each other in Margaritaville, that 14 man berthing area on that giant rusty piece of white steel. We berthed together in the barracks.

Sheen took off to "A" school in Petaluma when I left for my school in Yorktown. After failing to get orders to be an Airedale, I found the next school that had an opening. It happened to be mechanics school, which was enough for me, to just leave as soon as possible. A trip across country was something to fantasize about, a different ocean over there. Though we had fought, we were still like an elderly married couple. Leaving Sheen was tough. I had watched so many others come and go, friends, shipmates, strangers, assholes, clowns – some waiting to die, some drunk, some gone before they left. When Sheen left, he never looked back. He never said bye. It was never acknowledged by anyone.

I wanted to celebrate our two years together. He seemed too busy. Avoidance. He never reached out, returned a call, or wished me fair well. He was gone.

When I left, I stayed. Having received orders for "A" school, I found an interesting offer at hand. The BM1 approved 30 days of leave/vacation, which I had stored up since arriving at the ship. The opportunity was too good to pass. Soon, I had checked off of the ship and out of the barracks and had "left" for my leave. Yet, I stayed.

Now staying with Gilmour and Bluejay. My intention was to hang out for a week and convince Katherine to travel across country with me. In my Ford Ranger, it could take us a few weeks to do it. Katherine said she'd think about it. And she did. She also avoided me while "thinking," *which was our style* – I told myself. I was ignorant, and though my friends encouraged me to go enjoy myself, I did little else other than drink myself into a stupor each and every day.

As the end of my 30 days approached, Katherine gave me word that she would not accompany me, and that she had little interest in me in any manner. Left aloof, and lonely, I realized I'd be driving across the country solo. I took to the bottle even harder and it began to take its toll on my body. Each morning I'd awake in a horrible state. Dehydration. Stomach pains. I'd start the day pounding water, then puking. My head would throb and spin for hours. One morning I went through my vomiting process and started brushing my teeth, I farted and a bunch of undigested food fell out of my asshole onto the floor. I started vomiting profusely in disgust. Curled into a ball in the bottom of the shower.

I spent one last weekend in San Diego, with Gilmour and Bluejay and whoever else was there in those days. We drank like we were at a First and Last Chance Saloon. Celebrated nearly two years aboard the Thrill. Arrived an upbeat Seaman Apprentice, leaving a disgruntled drunk. In those later days, in San Diego, I was fearful of going to Tijuana, and the beaches and bars were a hassle. My interest was to drink and debauch with my boys, my shipmates. So, in the course of my 30 days of leave, I spent 26 days in the barracks, with a view of the industrial Navy obstructing the beautiful Pacific and a light house that never flashed in my direction.

The timer was down to 4 days, it was Thursday. Sheen was gone. Georgia was gone. Shipmates had come and gone. Gilmour and Bluejay, wanted the best for their friend, and they catered to my needs. We drank. They said I should just go. To drive and not look back. My last day in town I had acquired a point of meth from Stagger and after snorting it over the course of an evening, I jumped in my truck and drove straight through to Yorktown, and checked into my school on Monday morning.

PART TWO

"A" School

"Do you know the only value life has is what life puts upon itself? And it is of course overestimated, for it is of necessity prejudiced in its own favour. Take that man I had aloft. He held on as if he were a precious thing, a treasure beyond diamonds or rubies. To you? No. To me? Not at all. To himself? Yes. But I do not accept his estimate. He sadly overrates himself. There is plenty more life demanding to be born. Had he fallen and dripped his brains upon the deck like honey from the comb, there would have been no loss to the world. The supply is too large." (London, 1999)
– Jack London. The Sea-Wolf

SHIPMATES

YARN 40
MK1 GORDON

He who dares to teach must never cease to learn.
—Richard Henry Dana Jr.

Gordon was the perfect personality to organize and teach our group of eclectic non-rates. He was young, knowledgeable and charismatic. In the first few minutes of our first class, it was apparent the school would be very different than other areas of the Coast Guard. Our working chain of command stopped at an MKC[74], who we would only see for administrative purposes. Otherwise, the MK1 was our only supervisor. He had the authority to pass and fail us. The Training Center enforced "marching rules[75]," and the MK1 preferred to not march, so he allowed us to report in civvies most days.

Obviously a history nut, Gordon seemed more like a National Park's interpreter than a Coastie, which was fitting at the Training Center in Yorktown, sandwiched between the York River and the Yorktown Battlefield. I began to relax into the setting, glad to be off of my extended leave, glad to be off the Thrill, appreciating the humid hum of Coastal Virginia. I pushed a mental reset button as I

---

[74] MK: Machinist Technician. The engine room experts.
[75] Marching Rules: established procedures, for uniformed personnel to move in formation. Single file, or as units. Cadence calling is necessary for larger units.

161

listened to my classmates give brief introductions. I gave mine in two sentences. And then MK1 Gordon gave his...

SON OF A GUN

"My name is PorJack Marshal Gordon, and I'll be your instructor for the next few months. My Great-Great-Great-Grandfather (PorJack) was a merchant mariner on cotton ships, back when the British wouldn't allow the colonies to produce their own textile fabric. His schooner's route was from Charleston to Bristol, and onwards to Western Africa (to use Africans as ballast on the way back home). During the outbreak of the Revolutionary War, My Great-Grandfather's ship was boarded by the Continental Navy, of the newly formed United States of America, and he and his shipmates were pressed into military service. For the 18th century unskilled mariner, this meant being thrown and locked in the gundeck. The gundeck on a man-of-war, in 1775, consisted of a 40' long deck with 4' high ceilings. Cannons would line both sides of the ship, ready to roll athwartship to their respective gun portals. Sailors pressed into service were not given the benefit of the doubt, and were often locked in this tiny area for as long as they were needed for the war (food and water

being fed through portals[76] in the deck). There PorJack lived for months, rarely encountering the enemy, but ready to load and fire the cannon on command.

"In need of orders and provisions, PorJacks's ship, the USS Man-of-War, pulled into New York Harbor. The officers on deck followed the customs of the day and contracted prostitutes (and/or forced poor women) to give the men in the hold their services. The women would then be locked on the gundeck for a useful amount of time. The off spring of such unions are considered "Sons of Guns." And that's how my blood line started.

"The story continues within the harbor, as an explosion sent my Great Grandfather's ship to the sea floor. The survivors of the wreckage were picked up by the enemy, the English, and pressed into service once again, on the opposite side. PorJack however was in no physical condition to serve, having received major injuries to his legs. Instead, the British set PorJack to work at a local light station (what eventual became the Montauk Lighthouse). With a Sailor's background, the British believed he would be an asset to help assist ships navigating the Coast. With prearranged light signals, PorJack could distinguish the ship's flag and intent from a horizon away. The British ordered him

---

[76] Portal: Corrupted form of Port-Hole. A hole in a ship built to easily transfer cargo to and from a ship while in port.

(a seemingly sympathizer of the Crown) to give light direction to the English, and no information to the Americans. He did the opposite.

"To tie this story together, as PorJack manned his light station, he was in a position which often witnessed shipwrecks. He developed a system to alert the local town's people during these awful events, to help rescue drowning passengers. This series of operations (lighthouse keeper to life-saving service) is the exact expansion of operations the US Coast Guard followed twenty years later (1790 – 1915). During one terrifying episode, when a passenger vessel ran aground during a storm, PorJack's call to the townsmen brought men and women. Amongst the responders was his dear lady-of-the-gundeck, with child in hand. In a strange twist of fate, he married his gundeck lover and took his Son-of-a-Gun as his own (which it may have been).

"The happy ending was not to be. Before the war stopped PorJack was found guilty of treason to the crown. He was hung on a gibbet by the entrance channel to the Hudson, for all sailors to see.

Gordon's family since has been either in the sailing industry or the prostitution one. The MK1's goal in the Coast Guard was to get stationed as the light house keeper at the Montauk Lighthouse (which turned out to be in vain, as the Coast Guard either privatized lighthouses or leased them to the National Parks Service in 2009[77]).

---

[77] With the technological advent of wireless and satellite communications, more and more private, commercial and industrial boaters are using private aids to navigation sources. The first major impact of this was the regulation of navigation equipment on the bridge of commercial vessels. Technology like radar, AIS (automated information system) and VHF are all now mandatory, as per CG regulations. Additionally, more useful technologies like electronic charts and smart phones have completely ruled out the need for many old Coast Guard aids to navigation, like light ships and loran C. As the rate of technological progress continues, the Coast Guard will reduce physical structures (which often occupy premium and valuable property) and archaic ATON. Lighthouses will become only tourist destinations for my mother's flock. Buoys will drift away. Paper charts will be stowed beside the sextant.

YARN 41

ASHORE, FN

The fishing pier at Yorktown reached far enough out into the York River to see the Chesapeake Bay. A can buoy, number 5, sat off the end of the pier, and with a constant flow of water east, had a permanent list[78] to that direction. During the work week I'd use the pier as an escape from the bar scene, which was just as exhausting as the barracks scene in San Diego. I'd met a non-rate, FN Avani, just out of boot but was old enough and lonely enough to buy me booze. After a few weeks at school we acquired fishing poles, and we would sit on the pier and cast out to the green number 5, for anything that would bite, mostly sting rays.

The humidity and rolling storms inflicted beautiful havoc on my senses. Every cicada, thunder roar, and overturned maple leaf would grab some distant personal experience and force it to replay in my mind. It'd been two years since I'd left Virginia. Reminiscing was inescapable. As I stared off, over the wooden railing, towards the river, Avani would get the clue to leave.

The oceans were an hour and a half away, the mountains about the same. My mother was from the Appalachian Mountains, so as a kid I spent more time there than at the beach. I loved both, though the suppressed access to the beach created a nostalgia

---

[78] List: A lean of a vessel caused by internal forces (like unbalanced cargo). Heel would serve as a better word here, though it doesn't resonate as nicely. Heel is a lean caused by external forces, like wind.

for it. Each year we'd load up the huge 15 passenger family van and drive south, swaying each time my father would swerve to pass a slower car, to Ocean Beach, on the southside of North Carolina, and bunk in a house full of distant relatives. My father did not "believe" in air conditioning, so the approach to the beach was full of wonderful smells. The ocean, just like anything you're not accustomed to, had attributes that seemed faraway and hard to name. Looking back, approaching the beach-house as a child was similar to a drunk approaching a bar and anticipating a drunk—subtle but true. The signal that good times were fast approaching was the smell of salt and sand – lowtide. On a conscious level, I was in awe of every aspect of the coast line – each grain of sand, the tides, waves, horizons, skies, sounds, birds, fish, people, stores, the ocean, the ocean, the ocean.

My desire for sea was not lost throughout the year. On my parent's land we had a creek and a pond. My brothers and I were limited to the types of entertainment we had, so fishing was a natural favorite. This fishing interest carried onwards to other ponds, lakes and rivers. The ability to navigate in dense woods, and therefore navigate in general, was something I educated myself on in the backcountry and rivers of Virginia.

As I aged, the ideas religion presented, and the way it grew over societies like ivy or like herpes, grew more and more appalling. Not able to sport false and dehumanizing beliefs, I started looking for another spiritual release. One that would be more productive. No tools in the Bum Fuck[79] to guide. No literature readily available. I turned to bedroom philosophy and conscious conscious change. And I began to delve deeper with any information I could get. Music – the

---

[79] Bum Fuck: a proper noun (and I'll fucking fight you if you say otherwise), used here to denote a sense of bottled anger towards the backwoods and outdated culture of my childhood home, Goochland County Virginia.

60s. Books – the transcendentalist. Sex– absolutely none. Acme – yes. Penis in my hand – multiple times a day.

Once I was goofing with some good friends on the fall line of the James River in Richmond. In that area the James drops some 105 vertical feet in the course of seven miles. This lends itself to great rapids, swirling pools, and high-school kids doing unwise activities. It also lent itself to my group of friends traversing below a dam there. The dam rose 20' off the lower river level. Continually, by the second, millions of gallons pour over that damn. A tremendous amount of force propels the water a good three feet away from the concrete damn itself, leaving a "tunnel" from one side of the river to the other. Which is a great spot for kids on drugs to transit. And there we were, including Anna, in a bikini with her skin and breast, cruising along this trippy path. Once to the middle, it was decided we would dive head first through the surging cascade of water. One after another, we all jumped through, tossed and turned in the thunderous whirlpool, and made it to the other side. Except for Anna. I saw her dive in, *saw her swirling around, saw her to continue swirling around.* I thought not. Jumped into the roaring falls. She was there, stuck in current limbo. I reached out and grabbed her arm, found my foot on a hard surface, and pushed the both of us down stream towards our oblivious friends. Anna held me, with her bikini breast against my chest and her lips close to my face: "oh my god thank you."

Months later Anna had sent me an invite to a house party in the mountains on a lake. Many of my friends were going and I couldn't miss it. Soon after that party I had found my life's mission, my purpose, and my journey.

t was dark. Lake Anna was nearly two miles in circumference, lined with tall skinny pines. Two lights were at play: the moon was up, dimmed by lacy translucent clouds, and there was a perimeter light on a flag-pole at the far side of the lake. I was swaying on a rocking-chair, I think, but maybe it was just a rocking chair, or standing, I don't know. I was in a state of euphoria. "Paint by numbers morning sky, looks so phony[80]," not completely accurate.

I was staring at the ripples on the lake, the water, the water, the water. The distant perimeter light bounced beams of white off the lake. The pines dark on the other side. The blue moon light at rest on the lake's ripples, changing in ascetic pastels in slow motion waves. *A wooden dock* in front of me, like I'm about to speed down it on snow skis. Rocking. Somewhere in this concoction of thoughts and euphoria my brain was imprinted with those ripples: *RIPPLES REFLECTING LIGHT EQUAL EUPHORIA.* The sounds of my friends swarmed by me. *Rocking.* The warm air in that part of the country lasts all night. You can sit naked on a dock and rock in a static chair. Play Dead albums in your head. Your arms wave accordingly. And stare at ripples as they turn orange, pink, purple and blue with the music. Rocking. *The sensation in the gut is too strong.* Friends running. People Yelling. Joe in my face: "We're swimming to the island!" *More running.* People not unlike blurs of color. Sound to my left and to my other left, like color. Anna, "Ashore, come with me. Come swimming with me. We're going to the island." I find myself on the end of a

---

[80] See The Grateful Dead's "Touch of Grey." (Dead)

wooden dock. *A wooden duck? "Where am I?"* I jump in. The water is in slow motion. I am in slow motion. *Bubbles. Bubbles everywhere.* My euphoric peace and interest gone. Now there is only silence knocking at my creative brain. *What's this do-something sensation? Do what?* I watch the chaos of water about me. A splash there. A single bubble in dark space. All in deliberate and lingering motion. An image of Anna's face. I can hear her shout my name. And my name again.

"Help," she shouts. "Ashore needs help!" She's frantic. "Swim!!!!!!"

YARN 42

SA AVANI

We established a working relationship. I'd give him rides every so often and he'd buy me liquor for the Training Center's fishing dock. In late spring and early summer, rolling thunder showers would appear almost daily, in and out within a few minutes. Humidity was as high as the temperature, 95, 100 degrees. Driving down the back roads, paralleling the river, I'd have to whack Avani's hand away from the AC controls. "I want to feel the air I'm driving in."

One unfortunate aspect of my experience in the Coast Guard was a communal lack of excitement for the neighboring world. On the Central Coast, Mayan pyramids were near every port-call[81]. A quick hop, skip and jump would have landed a flock of my shipmates in an ancient wonderland. Other port calls had similar destinations. Each and every moment, the world went by, and my friends and superiors found close bars to make it go by in a blur. Driving through the old Battlefield in that part of Virginia, my interest was sparked, and Avani seemed to be up for a history lesson.

---

[81] Port-call: a temporary stay of a vessel while on a prolonged deployment.

A HISOTRY OF THE YORK RIVER

Various tribes of Indians traversed the York River, heading to the Chesapeake in sleek canoes under paddle. The Powhattan go down on record as the first settlers, only because that's what the first English settlers decided to record (it's dumb to think there were no other groups here before the 16th century Indians). Otherwise, we know that the rivers of Virginia and the Chesapeake were inhabited by a multitude of other groups of Indians. By the very first decade of the 17th century, the English settled nearby. Their ships were much larger, but not as sleek. Originally in Jamestown, a short 5 miles from Yorktown, on the James River, the first English settlers lacked the skills and knowledge needed to survive in the low swamp lands of Virginia. They started dying off, and by sheer force of numbers (one ship after another for 200 years) they beat their death lot. Immediately they went to work on agriculture. The York River became a more useful port, due to its depth, and Yorktown was established and became a tobacco center. Over the next few decades the Norfolk/Jamestown/Yorktown area became the hub of trade for the English in the New World. Williamsburg was established. By 1680s, the problem of pirates became a reality for Virginia. Pirates were flourishing due to the bad economy, new technology, and chaotic and sparse enforcement of law and order. Edward Teach used the York River as a staging area for sacks on nearby villages. He even confessed to burying treasure at the mouth of the river (this, plus Drake's account, is one of the few documented cases of Pirates actually burying treasure). Just off of the present-day public dock in Yorktown, Teach (aka Blackbeard) would sail his gundecked[82] ships under the cover of dark and pick off weary travelers. Fast-forward 100 years and the Ally and British forces were bombarding each

---

[82] Gundeck: 1) to manipulate or lie on a ship's log. 2) Originally, to create fake gun portals on the side of a ship, to trick the enemy into thinking you have more guns than you actually do.

other. Yorktown Battlefield shows the pure idiocy of 18th century fighting. And though it is shameful to see, it is a perfect representation of an officer class puppeteering an enlisted (militia) class in the name of honor and style. Washington of course won the day here, and the New Virginias (used to be English) were freed to release their own kind of wrath on the Old World Virginias (Indians). The river kept flowing and soon there was another tremendous battle, this time in the 1860s. The States couldn't agree on the constitution's language, and the Southern States established their own constitution. While both states saw their own kind (white people with penises) as superior, the North was mad at the South because the South enslaved black people. Instead of defending its institution, the South defended its right to create its own laws (i.e. enslaving black people). The North sent a flotilla of ships to blockade all Southern ports and to blow up all southern boat yards. In the Chesapeake, there were numerous narrow deep-water channels available for the Confederacy to build and protect their ships. They set sail their first Ironclad[83] steam powered ship from the James River, and sent a smaller fleet down the York River to cause a distraction. From our vantage point in York Town we would have seen black men being whipped in the cotton fields, and heard thunder from the gun battle miles away. Fifty years later and the Union had established its largest Naval Base at the mouth of the Chesapeake Bay. Another fifty years go by and Fishing fleets, recreational fleets, Cargo and Tanker fleets all move in and out of the Chesapeake Bay and her rivers. Avani and I sip Jack and, on the banks of the muddy York, think about it all.

---

[83] Ironclad: Built in the mid 19th century, they were put to use first, and successfully, by the Confederates in 1861. A steam powered wood ship, covered in iron armor.

YARN 43

FIREMAN RED

The entire thing was a side gig for Red. A moment before class, and a moment after, he switched modes, from Coastie to Red. It was impressive, I have to admit. Born in Virginia, about an hour from my hometown, Red had a social networked established and he drove an hour home after school each day. His fiancé worked at a local Hooters near the Naval Base in Norfolk, and when the invitation was open, we'd all head that way after class to stare at her boobs and sneak vodka into our drinks. Not that Red would condone such a thing. He was adamant about staying out of our drama, he wouldn't buy us booze, and he wouldn't hang out if we began to get rowdy.

There was something to learn from Red. I was too naïve to figure it out.

He served on a Buoy Tender before our school. He and I were one of the few who had spent any time operational in the Guard. Everyone else in the class was straight out of boot. As a Black Hull Coastie, a term for Coast Guardsmen serving on buoy tenders (and ATON[84] units), Red's stories were all about mishaps. Anchor block not secured to the deck. Chain broke free during davit ops. Buoy drifted station into the breakers. Boat hit buoy. Wave broke over work deck and sent him and friends washing towards the gunwales[85].

I listened with great intrigue and tried to picture myself on a black hull. There was no fantasy there for me. My imagination forced open sea, law enforcement, or, under stress, third world gutters, cages, and sorrow.

---

[84] ATON: Aid to Navigation (buoy, lighthouse, dayboard, etc...)
[85] Gunwales: the side of the ship that transcends the height of the hull and deck. The term is the corruption of "gun" and "wale." The first in reference to a ship's cannon, and the second to the side planks of a ship – wale. Literally, the place on the ship's side where the gun rest.

JOURNAL ENTRY

Dana describing the struggles of a sailor by bunking in the forecastle was like a 19th century psychologist describing the struggles of a prostitute by measuring her skull. And with his measurements, he went home to his old money and prestigious institutions. Wrote poetry, reflecting on his meager moment as a working man. Was awarded for his poems. Wrote manuals for mariners, maritime terminology, maritime law. Was awarded for his views. Buddied up with the educated and the wealthy. Was awarded with friends in those places.

If money is a measure success, Dana was born successful. What a stupid way to measure success.

If experience is a measure of success, Dana's was as an impersonator. His famous reflection was based on a pseudo-experience. Ha! What a stupid weight.

If being swept away with life, in a feverish splendour is a measure of success. Maybe Dana was hot for it on the Pilgrim, or more so on the Alert(?). He certainly couldn't let it go.

YARN 44

RAMBO, FN

The thought of two more years in the Guard was unbearable. After the Thrill, I felt worthless and had regrets about enlisting. Watching the other guys have all the fun was too much for me. If I went back to a ship as an engineer (MK), I would never be on a boarding team or a law enforcement team, and I would probably never serve in operations. Mechanics School offered very few options for adventure seeking sailors, and I began to feel defeat.

1/5th of Jack in his gut, no vomit - carried on with his evening. At 5'11, 205 lbs, Rambo was solid muscle. With an idol like Arnold Schwarzenegger, nothing from Rambo should have been a surprise to me, but, as it unfolded, it was.

When I first met him in Yorktown, Rambo wore a white undershirt with the words "Rambo Rules" written on it in black magic marker. He wore the same shirt each day the MK1 allowed us to report in civvies. There wasn't too much time to socialize during the days, though afterwards, those of us who were single headed out to the nearest bar. Being underage, Rambo and I had to develop an elaborate way of sneaking in. When successful, we'd continue to that bar each night to establish trust with the bartender. And there Rambo and our friends were, at a pool hall in Norfolk, drinking and enjoying each evening in peace.

SHIPMATES

One particular night at our bar, we had a bottle of Jack. Always the antagonizer, Rambo was pressuring us to drink quickly. Between three of us, we were shit faced before the bartender served us a round. I wanted to finish the night early, so I put a cap on the evening and caroused everyone into my truck. I was anxious about doing well at the unit's physical fitness test and run the next morning. It would either open doors or limit options of which units we'd get orders to after school.

Driving through the dense tree-lined curvy roads seemed to be a challenge. The oncoming headlamps were not as bad as the two obnoxious passengers making boisterous jokes of everything. Rambo handed me the bottle. "I can't man, I'll puke."

Both passengers started chanting, "Chug! Chug!". As always, I folded under the peer pressure, grabbed the bottle and killed its contents. It went down, mixed with a bunch of beer foam, and started rising fast in the back of my throat.

"Grab the fucking wheel!" I yelled as I rolled down the window. I kept my foot on the gas, pushing about 50mph, on a busy backroad in the dark, and I leaned as far out as I could and puked in the wind.

Returning to the wheel I could feel the slime all over my cheeks and chin. Looking down I could see it actively drip off of my face onto my shirt. "We can't go through the i.d. check on base like this," I moaned to my laughing passengers.

While inside a 7/11, looking for some paper towels and cleaner, a cop pulled up and placed his headlights on my truck. We walked out of the store and tried to play it cool.

"Where you guys headed to tonight?"

I worried the Virginian cop was going to harass us due to my California plates, so I said my hometown "Goochland." As I said this I started hiccoughing. Everyone was silent.

"And who's driving?"

"Oh, I'm driving," I volunteered casually.

The cop shook his head. "Be safe out there fellas. There's a lot of bad drivers this time of night," and he walked away. I quickly scrubbed the chunks off the side of the truck and we took off for base.

M y sights were set on new units within the Coast Guard, MLEUs. They were supposed to be the combat units of the guard. Newly established by the DHS after 9/11. Lots of training and lots of deployments, and the possibility of going overseas. At "A" school, I exercised harder than ever in hopes of landing orders to a MLEU, and Rambo was the natural partner in this endeavor as he had a work out regiment down.

The morning after I vomited out of the truck window, we woke at 0600 to a physical test. This included a mile and a half run and a bunch of sit-ups and pushups. Walking to the start-line I kneeled behind a parked car and hurled. I was sure my gut would rip open. As I threw up, Rambo laughed. During the run he finished first and I came in nearly last.

This difference in body mechanics plagued me for a long time. I was often around alcoholics who were 100% functional during and after a night of complete debauchery. After six rounds, my brain turns off, memory fails, and I awake in strange places having done some of the most unbelievable things anyone could do – I am an animal on alcohol. This failed run was due to drinking. This failed run set me at the second-to-last spot on the list for post-graduation unit choices. I was devasted and I stumbled back to the barracks to continue puking and sit in sorrow at the bottom of the shower.

Weeks later, when orders came out, I was second to last to pick, out of 30 class mates. There were two units that fit the description of MLEUs (where I wanted to go) – one in Miami and one in San Francisco. The likelihood of me getting one of these positions was nothing. The possibility of me getting sent to a cutter or buoy tender in the Great Lakes or Alaska or the Mississippi River were high. I felt like shit and sat at muster as the MKC went through the roster of names.

Holy Shit. With three units left, at place 27 on the list, there was still a MLEU available! No one wanted to go to a Law Enforcement Unit!... But of course, number 28 took the spot. The last two billets were on the USCGC Mackinaw, in upstate Michigan, a buoy tender. *At least there'll be heavy drinkers there.* I meandered my way to my berth one last time. The following day was graduation, and we were expected to be in full dress uniform to go through that ceremony.

Before our last morning muster, I was called to the MKC's office, along with one other shipmate, the number 30 on the list (the guy who did even worse than me). We were a little worried and thought our poor grades in class were going to get us in trouble. When the chief said that number 28 was having his orders revoked, because he was caught cheating, and that his orders were open for us to pick, I almost shit. Without thought, I yelled "I'll take them!" In an instant my life course changed. I was going to an elite team in the Coast Guard! I would get my adventure after all.

The new orders were for San Francisco, and I was more than eager to go, even though I'd sworn off California from my days on the Thrill. Rambo had orders to that base too, as a shoreside engineer for the cutters home-ported there. We were going to be seeing a lot of each other. In the meantime, I needed to sober up and prep myself for my new unit. I parted ways with my "A" school comrades and off I went for a second 30-day solo vacation.

JOURNAL ENTRY

(October 2004) I made it through Yellowstone yesterday. I arrived at night and was driving before eight this morning. I'm at some gas station in Oregon now, some asshole won't let me pump my own gas. He greeted me at the pump when I was clearing out all my piss bottles...

The things you can learn on the road. Go figure... A billboard in Missouri taught me Samuel Clemens' pen name, Mark Twain, means "barely navigable waters." On the Mississippi, where he was a pilot, a leadsmen would shout the term at two fathoms, which I guess would be shallow for the vessels Twain was driving.

Those Missourians know nothing about Jack London! His name is better. It was John London – London taken from his step-father. John's biological father left his mother while she was pregnant with John. She shot herself in the head (while pregnant) at the thought of being a single mother in the horribly religious (judgmental) era of the 19th century. Jack finished the job 40 years later with the help of alcohol and morphine and a roller coaster of a life!

SHIPMATES

PART THREE

The MLEU

"Disgusted, sick, I turned away, and leaned over the rail, and looked down into the water." (Dana, 1840) – Richard Henry Dana Jr.

SHIPMATES

YARN 45

MR. S.

Never had I'd been more committed to doing good. Each Coast Guard experience I had thus far was in my wake. The orders to that elite unit were the perfect reason to straighten myself out. I would excel, grow, conquer!

Leaving Yorktown, I had more vacation on the books. I took it all in route to my new permanent duty station in San Francisco. For a third time, I traveled solo across the country, this time taking it slow, no meth brain. I left the South as soon as possible, drove north for Chicago, the Dakotas, then west across the plains, meandered into the Colorado basin, then to Yellowstone. With a camper shell on the back of my truck, I slept on the move, absorbed the country as I went. Small bum-fuck towns, littered with churches. Cities, littered with churches, mosques, and temples, people underneath the bridges downtown. Then the woods, *the woods, the woods. Mountains and rock.* Deer. Birds. Deserts. Through Idaho and along the Dalles, where Lewis and Clark once sailed. Down the immense Columbia River Gorge, all the way to Astoria. The Pacific. I'd seen her from out there, never from that latitude on the beach. I was swaying on the shore, watching it, the ripples turn to roaring breakers. Light reflecting in harmony with its movement. The Coast of Oregon, into California. Snaking along highway 1, like a seabag on a luggage carousel, flipflop-heels together, toes at 45-degree angles. Cliffs prodding down into the sea-bubble-blue sea. Waves crashing. Wind. Constant blow of salt-stank into the nostrils. Woods. *The Ocean.* Feel a smile. *The Ocean.* San Francisco.

M ore pipelined meetings with people of authority. The Captain was in an appointment, but "he sends his 'Welcome Aboard.'" I could choose my route. In the Engineering Department I could work with Support, and fix shit. In the Operation Department there were two divisions, Landside and Waterside: I could crew small boats and join Boarding Teams. Or, I could do ninja shit – jump out of helicopters, go through SWAT training and other combat and tactical instruction. I'd have to prove myself at each level. "Here, we don't have time to waste. You're either on the team or off it."

On day two at the MLEU[86], I was ushered into a Waterside and Landside security meeting at one of the old brick buildings on the Coast Guard base. Without knowing a face, I was pushed through the door, quickly introduced to the class, and told to find a seat. There were 50 plus people in the room.

The unit had formed a year earlier. Each pair of eyes looking at me belonged to a plankowner[87], Coasties that pioneered and launched the post-9/11 unit. After an intensive six-month training session at Camp Lejeune, they all loaded onto a C-130, and flew to their new home-base in San Francisco. They ordered a bunch of small boats, weapons, and tactical looking shit, and were in business. I was the

---

[86] MLEU: Maritime Law Enforcement Unit.

[87] Plankowner: the word was once used to label original crew of a wooden ship. That crew would have been present during the laying of the ship's planks. Today, the navy and CG uses the term to signify a unit member was present when the unit/ship was commissioned.

first new guy since they started, replacing a mechanic who had been discharged for failing to meet the physical requirements. And there I was, 50 faces staring at me as I crab-walked my way to a vacant seat.

Mr. S. was in the front of the room. "Empathy is a step further than sympathy." *Wait, where the fuck am I.* "If you look at the definitions, you'll quickly see the difference is significant. If we can harness the implications of each of these terms, empathy as an emotion, and sympathy as a strategy, we can proceed to do our jobs better." *Ah.* I looked around the room, everyone was day dreaming. "The word 'but,'" and again I looked around. A few faces staring intently at Mr. S. and others looking at the floor. "'But,' is a negation word. If you use it in an order, when you're building a case for action, you need to understand how the word acts on the mind. Consider... [interrupted]"

BANG. BANG. *Firecrackers? What the fuck!* "Everybody get on the fucking floor! Get down! Get down! Get Down!" BANG!

A group of guys with pantyhose over their face flew into the room. One of them was holding a pistol and firing it into the ceiling. *Shit, am I peeing?* I looked around and everyone was on the floor. A guy next to me was smirking. Another guy had his eyes closed.

"Everyone look the fuck up here," shouted one of the perpetrators in an oddly fake Russian accent. Mr. S. was on his knees with a gun to his head. "Is this your superior officer?"

No one answered. Another armed guy moved through the crowd and jerked a Petty Officer[88] off his stomach to his feet, "answer the fucking question!"

"Yeah, Yeah," the PO said nervously.

The guy in the front of the class, with a seafarer's wide stance, pushed his pistol deeper into the face of Mr. S. "You will tell me the

---

[88] Petty Officer (PO): synonymous with an enlisted rank from step 4 to 9: E4, E5, ..., E9. Enlisted rank below all officers and warrants.

names of everyone in the room as I point to them. If you stutter, I will shoot this man in the face. Begin!"

The Petty Officer looked panicked, and he started stuttering, "uh, uh," he pointed to the guy beside him and said "Petty Officer Nolan Creavey."

Some of the guys beside me started laughing. Then someone started flicking the light switch on and off and Mr. S. said loudly "Drill secured." I immediately put a hand to my crotch. It was dry.

YARN 46

RED, MK3

R ambo wasn't the only one with orders to San Francisco. Our friend Red was there as well, reporting to the same unit as Rambo. All new personnel arriving to the area report first to a small building on the Coast Guard Base called "the Barracks," which doesn't sound like a clever name, but if you see the building it is a bit more ironic. The Barracks was only good for very short-term stays, about a week. When I arrived, after my 30-day post-school leave, I walked straight into Rambo and Red there. It was surprising to see them, as I thought this base would be too big to easily run into people you know.

This was the moment that sealed my destiny at my new unit. We all look for comfort in the face of change, so I naturally started hanging out with Rambo and Red when I wasn't at my new post. We lived in the barracks for about three weeks and we were able to solidify our friendship once more waiting for orders to move into the nearby military housing.

My new unit mustered at 0530 each morning for workouts. From 0600 to 0900 we had orders to do physical exercise that would help us in our jobs at the station. At my stage, I needed to train generally to pass the more difficult PT test. Unfortunately, I was back to drinking with my old "A" school buddies. When we left morning muster, in our issued PT gear, I would "run" around the base, zig and zag between buildings, and eventually, when I thought I was out of sight, I would zag directly into the escape exit of the barracks, jog up the stairs to my dorm, deadbolt the door, and crawl into bed for two hours. I would then wake, take a freezing cold shower, not dry at all, put my running clothes back on, and sprint at high speed back to my unit. Where I would end up panting and wheezing in the parking-lot. With all that water dripping off of me and soaking through my clothes, it must have looked like I was working out in the most brutal of ways.

After work I'd stroll back to the barracks, Rambo and I would coerce Red into buying us beer, who was now lacking his social network. The three of us couldn't stand the boredom of base. Rambo and I went first, scouting for a bar we could call home while still underage. Then, once we found it, Red would join us. We had soon meandered our way through the local bar scene, and established relationships with all the right people. Our go-to became a small Irish dive we called Shammie Dammies. It was to become our second home, our hospice.

YARN 47
EM3 HUNTER

My strategy was to not make friends within my unit. I didn't want them knowing I was a drunk in my free time. The first exception to this rule was EM3 Hunter, who became a quasi-friend to me in my early days at the unit. Hunter was a golden child[89] at the unit. He worked in the Support Department, yet he was a diver and participated in small boat ops. When there was cool stuff to do, he did it, and when we were back at base, he kept busy working on the boats. He was also the physical trainer and coach for the waterside, which meant he led morning exercises and routines for the entire waterside department. After I first arrived and failed my PT test, he became my mentor. "You smell like you're hurting Ashore? If you want to make it, and you talk like you do, you have to figure out the drinking and smoking thing. First, switch to dip. Chew has no negative effects on your lungs, but you'll still get the nicotine. Second, if you drink, you gotta be willing to run the demons out, every morning, not just when you want to."

Hunter and I had a lot in common. Both of us were from Virginia and we both were active outside of our unit. While we didn't mind spending time with our team, we both found it safer not to. At some point Hunter and I started hanging out at local bars. He let me in on

---

[89] Golden Child: the mythical persona of one who will benefit all mankind, either through his warrior traits or god-like power. The classics are the children of God: Athena, Hercules... R.H. Dana silently paraded himself as a golden child.

his online dating addiction, where he would meet random women around the Bay and fuck them once and never see them again. He always had great stories, like one woman who insisted he cut her inner thighs with a hunting knife as they fucked.

When Hunter's tour ended, I had been at the unit for 6 months, and I was in a position to fill his shoes, which I tried my best to do. When he departed, I didn't have any comms with him other than email. The last message he sent me was that he was "in the market for a dog."

MR. S.

"*The number one thing you have to remember is the Use of Force Continuum.*"

"*The moment you arrive on scene you've entered into the use of force continuum. Level 1 is officer presence. You are the officer. Your presence is one of authority, and many people you interact with in the world will not respect that. Your job isn't to force people to respect you, it is to use the minimum amount of force possible to get people to listen to you. And what you are telling them is – well that's a different conversation. Present yourself first, and the rest will follow.*"

"*The 'Coast Guard' is an image we have to fight for. We wage war constantly on behalf of that image. That image protects you, it protects your shipmate. If there is nothing else you do for your country, as a member of the Coast Guard, protect that image.*"

YARN 48

BM3 SHIVERS

aw relaxed. Breath in. Breath out. No movement of the head. More breaths. A forced swallow. Now he's moving his tongue around his mouth before he speaks. *I know he's going to speak.* "Isn't this really cool guys? We're like Navy Seals or something."

"Shut the fuck up Shivers!" the Boarding Officer responded, "Fucking mouth breather."

Our boat crashed through the crest of an unexpected swell, flew off the other side, and fell five feet. Our lights were out, and so were all the other boats' lights. At 2300 hours we were due to converge on the entrance of Halfmoon Bay, where a known motorcycle gang member had a vessel moored. There was supposed intel that this vessel was being used as a meth lab. As we approached from sea, with six small craft, each carrying a boarding team of five, the landside-team advanced in from the shore, in white unmarked vans.

Twelve hours earlier we were all sitting in a conference room listening to the playbook for this operation. Never having many things to do, our typical operations included "deterrence" measures, which were sporadic patrols around our area of responsibility, near potential high interest targets. When "intel" got word of this suspected meth lab, the CO was able to articulate action under the newly established Patriot Act[90]. No warrant needed and no other

---

[90] Patriot Act: regulation which was swept into law during the first few days after 9/11, when everyone was very emotional. The regulation gives tons of power to federal law enforcement agencies, including the USCG, so long as they are "preventing terrorism." The most disgusting part of this regulation is its

reason than "suspect terrorist activities" were needed, to make boardings on any vessel at any location within the jurisdiction of the United States. This included inspections, arrest and seizures of property 100 yards from any shoreline, on vessels moored or at anchor. The intel we had, and the way our CO interpreted the Patriot Act, allowed us to use "suspect meth lab" as a "suspected terrorist activity."

Back to our vessel flying through the waves in pitch black, Shivers was excited. The coxswain on our vessel, BM3 Rossi, produced "Flight of the Valkyries" and turned the volume up. And for the first time, I felt like I was participating in something very non-American, the snowball started rolling. The BO started to go through the order of operations again. The boat slowed, and through the window we could see the outline of our other boats. The radar showed all of us in the shape of a flying V. The Halfmoon Bay entrance buoy was going by the starboard side. Its red light shone on Shivers' open face as he made some weird noise. Rossi turned down the music.

---

failure to define the terms. Law Enforcement units around the country have defined terrorism to include "efforts which support terrorism," which has come to include things like manufacturing, selling and distributing "illegal drugs."

YARNS 49 TO 52

CHARLES BLACK, FIREMAN APPRENTICE

He was the youngest of four Catholic brothers. His older brothers were legends in the Coast Guard. When Rambo and I met him, he needed a case of beer. On the way to play frisbee golf, we bought him his case and he drank it before we made the course. He actually drank it on the freeway, in traffic, in less than an hour. As we exited the freeway, Charles opened the door, much to our surprise, and started vomiting beer foam. "I need another case of beer."

JON BLACK, DC3

I don't know where to start with Jon. He is one of the most kind, caring, sweet, drunken, sailor-type of creatures one could ever meet. As one of the middle brothers in the Black family, he had a guaranteed chance at joining the Coast Guard. His success rate of being kicked out was pretty high too.

I don't recall meeting Jon. At some point I was just sort of living on his couch. He used to rub my back while I was puking, "you want another beer bud?"

There were a few rough nights at Coast Guard Single Housing, where the alcohol may have been too much (there was always a boat returning or about to leave – reasons to drink everywhere – it's Monday!). Jon and I used to buy boxed wine each Wednesday and spread Havarti cheese over French bread and have "Fancy-Pants Wednesdays." On one of these special days we had chased a cat into a random house. Cat hunting with butcher knives apparently. As we rounded the hallway corner and found ourselves in a stranger's kitchen, a husband-wife couple staring at us, we quickly shielded our giant knives behind our backs and apologized profusely. We back peddled out of there. On another occasion, I had entered a who-can-hit-harder match with my buddy Rambo. When my mandible became shattered and detached from my face, blood dripping out of every orifice on my head, Jon was there to rub my back again "hey there bud, you'll be alright. You wanna beer?"

ANTHONY BLACK, DC2

I didn't meet Anthony Black until I visited his brothers in St. Louis. Anthony was famous in the Guard because he had a water-tight hatch fall on his hand as he scaled down a ladder. The hatch severed four of his fingers and the officer-on-duty allowed him the curtesy to go to sick-call. The medic at sick-call almost threw up at seeing the spaghetti looking hand, then sent Anthony in an ambulance to the neighboring Airforce Base hospital. The hand was somewhat fixed by Air Force doctors. Now, Anthony has three fingers on his right hand that kind of work, though he says they are in constant pain. The other fingers are nubs, which stand out when he palms a beer.

Anthony was the second oldest of the four Black brothers, and he refers to me as the crazy German every time we meet. We spoke about VA benefits and "unfortunately," Anthony says, "the VA is a bitch to work with. I only was awarded 10% disability and I can't even hold a shovel, much less a welding torch."

"To successfully land VA benefits, as a Coastie, you have to hound the VA and never stop pursuing your case. If they say no. Apply again. When the DRO doesn't respond to your letter, write a second copy of it and cc your congressman. Never stop. We're all fucked cause of this shit. Some of us have problems we can see. Some of us aren't so lucky."

BUBBA BLACK, DC1

Bubba was the oldest Black brother. He followed his dad into the service, and when his father died young, Bubba decided to become a father figure to his brothers. He encouraged them each into the Guard, and as many a sailor family do, the Whiteys would then forever forward be sailors, drunks, and Catholics-by-birth.

YARN 53

BM3 POND

P ond was a machine. He had body dysmorphia, because he was made fun of as a kid for being fat, and ever since, he worked out a minimum of four hours each day. As part of the landside security team, dive team, and generally as a ninja, Pond was a motivating factor in my push to do more at the unit. In the locker rooms and on smaller deployments, I heard Pond talk about his adventures with women and late-night drunken depravities. Pond's words of encouragement to me were the same as Hunter's, to "run the demons out," which was a reference to working out harder if you have a hangover.

Pond could have a movie made after him. After the MLEU he went on to be an AST[91], which are the Hollywood heroes of the Coast Guard. But Hollywood would never publish the best story of Pond's

POND'S TACTICAL INSERTION

At a local bar in San Francisco, many of the MLEU crew had arrived at the same time, by coincidence. It was rare for so many of us to be drinking together, and amongst the party were both BM3 Shivers and BM3 Pond, who were not fond of each other in the least. The conversation was dominated by these two, and each time Shivers would speak, Pond would get

---

[91] AST: Aviation Survival Technician. Overly glorified position in the CG. CG public affairs uses the image of AST to represent the CG as a whole, which terrorizes the reality of the situation, and confuses the troops.

annoyed and say something derogative towards Shivers. At some point, Shivers left to use the head and he left his beer bottle sitting on the table. Without missing a beat, Pond dropped his pants, bent over, and inserted Shivers' beer bottle a solid inch into his asshole. He then sat the drink back on the table. The group all sat in amazement, processing what we just watched. Most of us actually saw the spit-lubricated penetration.

Shivers returned to the table and drank from the contaminated bottle. We all stared on in total and abhorrent awe as Pond fell to the floor laughing. He gained his composure after a long minute, stood up, leaned his elbows on the table and looked deep into Shivers' face. As Shivers sat with his mouth ajar, Pond confessed his deeds in the most as-a-matter-of-fact and descriptive way.

YARN 54

KAREN, RED'S WIFE

She reached towards me. "What about this? Does this bother you?" She grabbed my left shoulder. My stomach curled and my brain strained. I didn't know what to do. Touch was never my thing. "What about this?" She stroked my back.

"Please stop." I focused on the beer in my hand. Karen was obviously drunk.

She jumped on me. "Oh Ashore, just a little hug!"

With no control over my actions. I flew out of my seat, and Karen went flying to the floor in turn. "Get the fuck off of me, stupid bitch!" And I stormed out of the bar, and walked down the side walk, away from my friend who was just loving me.

YARN 55

BLUEJAY, FS3

Bluejay called complaining that our friend was marrying some bartender from Portland. He's worried we won't see him again. I think he's projecting his fears and anger towards Gilmour's wife. At the same time, I'm a little concerned Gilmour didn't tell me himself. He's like a brother. He better fucking tell me these things.

CAPTAIN

O ur unit was scattered around the base, in various buildings and trailers, thrown together in a hurry after 9/11. The one central location we had, to call our own, was a small grass area near our chief's office. Unit wide musters usually took place in the gym though, where we all mustered daily as a unit anyways, on the basketball court, at 0600.

> "OK team. We train hard. Each and everyone of you is a vital element to our goal. The saying 'as strong as the weakest link,' is more crucial here then anywhere. The orders we received yesterday haven't made it out of my office. And outside of Mr. S and Chief Raleigh, not a soul knows what they are. This is the way it will stay, for security purposes. I want you each to tell your significant others the truth, that you don't know where you're going. And I want you each back here in four hours. This is our chance to [A basketball dribble started at the far side of the court. Sneakers squeaking. Both echoing loudly.]...
>
> "This is the chance – The opportunity we've be training for. As we depart this base. You will each have orders sealed, you will open them in your given transport, only after you exit the base. We will merge on our destination separately, to minimize any attention a convoy would give. [The basket ball rolled into the middle of our team meeting

> and a big guy in little shorts apologized profusely as he
> excused himself to get the ball.]
>
> "Be back in 4 hours. Your section chiefs will tell you what
> to pack. Dismissed.

We all looked around to see each other's reactions. The faces were emotionless. Rossi and Pond ran towards the guys playing basketball and joined their game. The BMC said he didn't know what to pack either. BM1 O'Brien made some joke about his wife "PMS-ing anyways," so it was a "good time to head out of town."

YARN 56

KURTZ, BM3

O ur MLEU had departed San Francisco as individual units, in route to MLEU San Diego. Vans carrying crew last. The boats, staggered every 15 minutes. K9 and Weapons trailer, every 30 minutes. All before the sun came out, to clear the Bay Area before rush hour. A few tire issues and head breaks, and we were all flocked together before we hit the Grapevine[92].

Still a 3rd class. Still a BM. Still in San Diego. BM3 Kurtz was spraying down one of the boats when we pulled into the parking area. I stepped out of the F550. I looked at him. He looked at me, spit something foul on the ground, then sprayed it away the power washer.

I should have walked away but I couldn't help myself. "What's up BM3? How's that collar treating you?"

He looked down to his shirt. I couldn't help but cough out a laugh. He gave me an attempted mean look, a growl almost. I gave an overbearing smile.

---

[92] Grapevine: an area where highway 5 exits/enters the southern portion of California's Central Valley.

YARN 57

RED, MK2

They allowed me to lay my arms and head down at Shammies. Most bars kick people out for falling asleep or looking like your about to fall asleep. Not Shammies. They knew me.

The bar was forever sticky, with smeared beer, smeared liquor, and old bleach water. My arms crossed in front of me, my head restless on my elbows. I could read the notes written on the dollar bills tacked to the ceiling (Shammies was a First and Last Chance Saloon)[93]. An emptying pitcher to my right. A glass with six gulp-lines[94] beside that, empty. I could feel Red's presence near, behind me. He was talking to the cute bartender; he was always talking to the cute bartender. Sunday morning. Shammies hadn't opened yet, but we always arrived early to "help set up." Karen had disappeared to the bathroom. At that point I started assuming she was using some type of speed, though I never said anything to Red. The cottage cheese in my stomach, plus the fresh booze, was nulling the ulcer

---

[93] First and Last Chance Saloon: bars on the waterfront are the first establishment a sailor can get a drink upon return from sea. Likewise, they are the last chance at a drink before deployment. In the seagoing community, many times your vessel is on an opposite schedule as your friends, when you leave, they return, and vice versa. A First and Last Chance Saloon is a good place to buy your friend a drink, by writing his name on a $1 bill ($5, but this isn't the case anymore. Now we prepay the bartender and write a name on the board.) and tacking it to the ceiling. If a dollar remains on the ceiling for a prolonged amount of time, it is assumed a sailor was lost at sea. This tradition has turned plastic over the years, and dollars tacked to the ceiling are just another way for people to say "I was here."

[94] Gulp-line: You can tell how many sips it takes someone to finish a drink, by the foam lines formed on the glass. The fewer lines, the heavier a person drinks.

pains I'd developed months early. I got up to smoke. Red followed me outside.

Shammies is in the heart of Alameda, a small island–city in San Francisco Bay. Faces on the street all look familiar. A weather-worn and beaten homeless man shuffled across the street at the sight of me and Red leaning on the bar's window. "Mornin' Ashore, Red. Can ya spare a cigarette?" He was saying this as Red and I had already pulled out smokes and held them for Al to choose. He lived in a nearby bush and was just waking up to make first call at Shammies.

Karen's voice could be heard through the window, asking for a second mimosa. Red pulled out another cigarette and went to lite it, but stopped mid flame. "Hey Ashore, tell me about the girl from the Populus, the buoy tender. What's her name? Daisy? Is she pregnant? Is it yours?"

"That's a big question, Red... The short story is, who knows? The longer story is a bit more fucked up and I'm not really trying to reflect on it."

"You can't just knock someone up and walk away, dude. Even if she is a Coast Guard slut."

"I don't think she's a slut. Maybe. But I don't think so. We fucked a few times and then she just started clinging onto me. She won't stop calling. At least she's stationed on YBI[95], so I don't have to see her at work."

"Are you listening to yourself? Ah. Fuck it. You want a beer? It's on me."

Karen came out and asked for a cigarette. "You guys are talking about Ashore's new girlfriend huh? Is she pregnant! Hahaha! She's pregnant, isn't she?"

---

[95] YBI: Yerba Buena Island. The San Francisco Bay Bridge tunnels through YBI, a natural island in SF Bay. The neighboring, and attached, "island" is Treasure Island, which is manmade.

"Damnit. I don't know. I don't know anything about it. People need to keep their mouth shut."

Karen couldn't stop laughing. She was so good at poking my soft spots. "So you're going to marry her or what? Haha. Do you see her every day?"

"Damn it! No. I don't see her. I really don't give a shit what people say. It's fucking annoying. Damn it."

Red: "Alright man. Let's just drop it."

Karen whispered, "Little Por-J Jr. running around! So cute."

YARN 58

BM1 DONALDSON

It was late night out on the water. Our two boats zoomed across the bay on our normal patrol. BM1 Donaldson was our Boarding Officer, and he was the coxswain of my boat. As we rounded the North side of Alcatraz, we spotted a 40' sailing vessel without running lights on, and we adjusted our route to intercept.

"August West" was the vessel's name. It brought a melancholy smile to my face, but I knew it would be beyond my shipmates. On board was a couple in their 50s, enjoying their evening. When we pulled alongside, the man aboard was quick to be annoyed. Donaldson yelled out his window, "Your lights are off." The man disappeared into the boat and the running lights came on. When he popped back out Donaldson started going through his hippie-smasher routine.

"How many people do you have on board?"

"Is there a problem?"

"Sir, have you been drinking tonight?"

"I don't understand your questioning. My lights were off. I'm sorry. Now they're on."

"I asked if you've been drinking tonight. Sir, go ahead and maintain your course and speed, I am going to board your vessel. How many people do you have on board?"

Donaldson leaned back into our cabin and asked our gunner to take the helm. He whispered to everyone, "I bet these fucking hippies have drugs on board. Wanna do a bust?"

We all looked at each other and the general consensus was "yes."

Leave the people alone, you fucking assholes.

For our own safety, so the books say, we give each and every vessel a basic safety inspection. This includes an intrusive search of the vessel for possible water intrusion – "to ensure the boat is sea worthy while we are onboard." Our two boats sent four people to the August West, including myself. While the boarding team went through this inspection, Donaldson went through his set of questions.

"Do you have weapons on board?"

"No. And what gives you the right to be doing this."

"I'll ask the questions, sir. Do you have any drugs or contraband?"

The man pulled a bag out of his pocket, "Well I have this but I have my medical card to go with it."

"And what exactly is that?"

"It's about a quarter of medical grade marijuana."

"Sir, I'm going to ask you and your passenger to place your hands on your head for me."

"Wait, What! I said I have a medical card."

"Sir. The possession of marijuana is a criminal offense. I am going to have my officers accompany you until we get this sorted out. Petty Officer McFly, Petty Officer Ashore, can you two go through what we've been training on." He motioned to his hand-cuffs.

"Wait a second! You can't do this to us! I have fucking medical issues. I have a fucking doctor's signature on my card. I have fucking rights you fucking fucks!"

Donaldson was the personification of all that I was starting to despise about the Coast Guard.

YARN 59

J. MOSS, IT2

Rossi popped up to his knees, and piloted her body to face away from him. Doogie style was the first cue to the guys bird-watching from the closet. He was drunk, and he couldn't help but laugh. She was oblivious to what was going on, also drunk, though caught in the moment, where a muscular attractive guy was actually making sweet love to her. She couldn't wait to tell her friend Sara in the morning. "Would he let her sleep here?" She thought, as he thrusted from behind.

The guys in the closet (Pat, Jeremey the Jew, and Moss) were supposed to be watching, with silent patience. Though they were all like little boys, fighting for the slit in the closet-door to peep through. As soon as Rossi gave an Indian war-cry, the guys were supposed to jump out of the closet. Rossi was taking his sweet ass time, "probably waiting to cum," suspected Pat. If all worked perfectly, the signal would be hollered, the guys would jump out, Rossi would then grab the hips of the fat chick and hold on as long as possible, as the guys counted the seconds. If Rossi could beat Pat's record of five seconds, he'd win. I'd heard them talk in the locker room, calling the sex game "rodeo."

No one knew Moss was drunk, real drunk. They'd all been drinking of course, for most of the night in fact, though Moss didn't show any of his typical rowdy drunk symptoms. He was quiet, until

Jeremey the Jew got in his way, taking too long at the peep hole. Moss was a weight lifter and was able to forcibly fling Jeremey out of his way. Jeremey and Pat were startled in the dark corner of the closet. They both saw the lack of jest in Moss's movements. Pat started fuming. Jeremy the Jew spoke up, "Dude, chill out man." Within nano-seconds Moss shoved Jeremey through the closet door, spilling himself into the bedroom. Rossi and the girl jumped off the bed. Moss sprang up, "You fucking took too long, Rossi. Fuck! God Damn it!" And he stormed through the house. Everyone was left staring dumbly. The girl quickly grabbed her things, with a fearful expression on her face.

O ut in the night, Moss drove. No one knows where he went, and neither does he. There is a three-hour gap between him leaving that house and when the police found his body. The two cars at the scene were so mangled it wasn't obvious who hit who. Both bodies they found were unconscious, though Moss was thought to have a higher chance of survival, so the first responders focused on him, leaving the mother-of-three to die in a nearby ditch. It took days to sort everything out, and Moss wasn't much help recalling the facts. The mother was driving home from a late shift. Moss was in the wrong lane.

J. Moss, IT2

JOURNAL ENTRY

(July 2005) I'm in a Motel 6 near Camp Lejeune. Elfkin and I were sent here to complete Tactical Boat Crewmen school. It poured on us today. We were engaged in M240 training at speed, and we could see the lighting in the distance. As the clouds passed overhead the instructors gave us the option to keep training or head in. The humidity was as thick as fog. That typical machoism is here, and without delay the guys all chanted to continue. Something about shooting an M240 is fun for people. I was entranced by the thickness of the air and lightning on the near horizon. My eyes were baited by the swaying pines, which lined the Intracoastal Waterway[96]. As I took my turn at the gun, I was entranced by the tracer rounds. I didn't care where they hit. They were beautiful in the dark musk. Tracers. Lightning bugs. Lightning. It's good to be back in the South.

---

[96] Intracoastal Waterway: An inland waterway, natural and manmade canals and channels, which provides shelter from oceanic conditions while traversing the southern states in a vessel.

YARN 60

ASHORE, PO3

t was another HIV security zone. The normal protestors at the base's main gate delayed our release. These protestors were not equipped with nude feminist[97] – no titties, no fun. We waited on station. Two 25's and the Command Center slightly up stream. The HIV was preparing to leave, so we heard, and the base and wharf were more alive with longshoremen.

Earlier a tug had approached our zone and we reached out on 13, "Tug Patricia Ann, what's your destination." Silence. "Tug Patricia Ann, Tug Patricia Ann, Tug Patricia Ann. This is the United States Coast Guard off your starboard bow, again, this is the United States Coast Guard off your starboard bow. You are approaching a security zone. Respond Channel 13." More silence. We all half expected the silence. It was always nearly impossible to contact the escort tugs on the radio. The tug captains didn't seem to give a shit about our orders, our zones, or our demands. They had real jobs to do. Then we tried on Channel 16: "Tug Patricia Ann. Patricia Ann. Patricia Ann. This is the United States Coast Guard, United States Coast Guard, United States Coast Guard, off your Starboard Bow. You must stop making way immediately until you are cleared to enter this security zone." No response. The coxswain became anxious and

---

[97] Many security zones the MLEU maintained in the first decade of the 21st century were accompanied by protestors. Feminist would often be amongst the protestors, topless. Accusing the patriarchy and testosterone as the evil of the world.

pulled our vessel in the track-line of the goliath tug. Rossi's phone was ringing non-stop during this and he finally answered it. We could all hear the voice at the other end. "Patricia Ann is hailing you on 13, idiots. Turn your volume up."

After the three-hour delay and the embarrassing tug incident from earlier, we were all ready to go back to the hotel, there was a bar there with a good juke-box. The bartender was a sweet old hag who wanted to sleep with all of us, though I'm not sure if any of us did, other than Pond. We were waiting, and the relief was saying they would be another 30 minutes. I snuck to the bow and bent down below the gunwales and lit a cigarette, and stared at the crystal-clear sky, swaying with the boat's motions. Abruptly, a double blast on a little fog horn sounded – "passing starboard-starboard." I stood up and first saw the startled look of Rossi's face, then the same look on the BO's face, I turned. A small power boat was moving at 5 knots about 50 feet off our bow. It was a Grand Banks with an older woman on the bow waving.

My first thought was that we had missed spotting this contact. Second thought was that the other two vessels missed this contact too. The third thought was that, if it was a hostile contact, and moving at any significant speed, it would have had passed us before we saw it. *BOOM!* But it wasn't hostile. I threw my cigarette into the scupper, stood up and motioned for the vessel to turn port and continue going. I could hear Rossi's voice on the radio with the Command Center. The vessel was a cabin cruiser, manned by an old retired couple, a completely normal thing to see in that part of the world. The woman shouted as they neared, "What are yall doin, huh? You're right in the middle of the river. Can't you give us some space."

I yelled back. "Ma'am, this is a security zone. Please have your coxswain maneuver your vessel to the North Side of the Channel."

"Well I just have no idea what any of that means." She shouted back to the man in the cabin, behind the helm. "George, do you know what he's sayin? I don't know what way North is."

I pointed to the far side of the channel. "Move that way. You do not have authority to enter this area."

She smiled and yelled loudly, now 20 feet off the bow, "oh alright. Well yall sure do look darling in your little uniforms and big guns. Thanks for the hard work. We'll just go the other way."

YARN 61
CHARLES AND JON

Rambo, Red and a group of Coasties organized a pirate-float for the local San Francisco Spring Parade, an eight-mile run/walk, called Bay to Breakers. The "float" was stolen from a lumber yard parking lot and was decorated with a keg and a cooler. Due to the nature of the track, through downtown San Francisco, volunteers were needed to help push/pull the cart up and down the city's infamous hills. Jon and Charles Black asked me to go and I said I'd drink on it.

Dressed in a speedo and floaties, lost and last, we pulled that busted cart for miles, behind 100,000 drunk and disgusting civilians. Through broken glass and urine, it was just a matter of time before we ditched. Charles went first, and he had a good excuse because he had lost his sandals a few miles before. His feet looked they just made it through Nakatomi Plaza. I went next. Looking for a bush, I wandered to a park and passed-out. I awoke to a burning sensation on my butt. Lying about 10 feet from third base, a group of parents and their kids were playing softball. My speedo had ridden down, exposing my right ass cheek to the sun. The sun burned a bubble on my ass and left a scar which is still with me to this day.

Reports came in the next morning that shortly after I left, the empty keg was replaced with Jon's unconscious body. He lay sprawled out on the steel-cart as Rambo and Red pulled and pushed him to the finish line by the Pacific Ocean.

A SHORT HISTORY FROM JON'S PONT OF VIEW

Jon was unconscious on the lumber cart, in the golden sands of Ocean Beach, just south of the Golden Gate Channel... Before Europeans arrived, the entire area of San Francisco was nothing but sand and dune. There's no natural water or vegetation on the northern peninsula, so it's no wonder the city itself lacks significant Native American History. But there Jon was - white skin tanning the color of Indian on the burning steel cart... Some 450 years ago, Sir Francis Drake sailed passed the Golden Gate Channel and landed about 20 miles North of San Francisco, in present day Drake's Cove, Point Reyes National Seashore. The flaming Protestant Drake would have hung Jon from a gibbet had he found him on the beach in such a heathen condition... The Spanish actually found the San Francisco Bay (which was a strange thing for them to claim, as thousands of people lived there when they arrived), and General Ayala placed the water-way on seafarer's charts, and he must have hoped the Sacramento River was the infamous North West Passage (it wasn't). The Catholic Spanish were floggers, and they would have whipped Jon to death for his sins (not recognizing his lineage)... Next came the Russian fur traders. Then the English again. Then Dana, who would have publicly disgraced poor Jon in his famous novel as "not a formidable man..." Then the gold rush. Sailing vessels and steam ships form Panama crammed into the Bay, landing directly against the shores of San Francisco. The city grew. The Mormons came. Then the Chinese. Then the Japanese, heavy with honor and tradition. They would have beheaded Jon... The Natives were burned, raped and baptized into oblivion... Jack London and Mark Twain came and went. Alcatraz was built, it's symbolic lighthouse. Then the Army Corps of Engineers, in a battle with the Bureau of Reclamation. The Beats. The queers. Then the hippies. Hunter S. Thompson showed – he would have thrown a bottle of water at Jon's head. Then the civil rights movement. The UC Berkeley Campanile[98] (also a lighthouse). Bridges. Aqueducts. Skyscrapers. Technology. Cell Phones. Smart Phones. Then, and currently, Jon Black's drunk unconscious ass half naked on a stolen lumber cart, and thousands of people just like him... Ocean Beach Bums, sitting and watching the great mariners of the world, in the Greatest and most Significant port that has ever been and will ever be!

---

[98] Campanile: a 300′ stone tower, 40′ squared. Built in the first decade of the 20th century. Locally, it is also known as Sather Tower. It can be seen from the Golden Gate, from its center look over the Alcatraz Lighthouse, and it is there like a giant range marker (which is on purpose).

YARN 62

ELFKIN, BM3

We never really talked until a deployment to the aftermath of Hurricane Katrina. News reports started rolling in, and within hours our Captain issued a recall. Before the day was up, we were on a C-130 to Baton Rouge. Elfkin and I were both preparing to qualify for BO Training School, so we talked over that topic on the flight. Once in New Orleans we combined assets for the cluster-fuck conditions.

Our unit arrived without detailed orders and without any knowledge of the area or the needs. We hitched a ride with the 82nd Airborne, on Humvees and troop transports, and rode into downtown New Orleans, looking like children whose parents just let them board bright red firetrucks. The Airborne had orders to report to a nearby shelter and they asked us to depart their escort, which we did near Canal St. A group of uniformed Coasties was there clearing a mooring area on the Mississippi for an approaching Coast Guard Cutter. We joined them and were soon catching mooring lines for the ship. That levee and adjacent quay became our headquarters for the next two weeks. We recruited a volunteer water truck (an 18-wheeler) that was manned by a retired husband and wife – the wife wore an American-flag tank top and the husband wore camouflage shorts and no shirt, hairy belly. We set up a half-assed decontamination center and fresh water center for residents in need. No one came, at all, the entire time we were there. We had lots of water, something the News said was in need. The Operations Officer of the Cutter allowed us to use the helo-hangar to spread out our sleeping bags. They couldn't spare the heads due to their inability to dump sewage over the past two weeks.

To escape the sea of sleeping bags and unshowered men, Elfkin and I found a dry-foods storage locker and made racks on the shelves. A local bar owner gave us a bottle of whiskey, and we celebrated our move from the helo-hangar to the dry-stores locker. I was sleeping when a chief came in. He was startled by us but he pulled himself together and acted as if nothing was the matter. He asked if he could reach behind me for a bag of potatoes. "I got a bag of potatoes for you right here chief."

A week later the amphibious Navy ship, the USS Iowa Jima, came to our dock and moored just in front of us. Suddenly we had all the food we could ask for, but Elfkin and I preferred MRE's to the Navy ship's galley. Showers were tough to come by, so we used the decontamination station at night when there was no one there to stop us. The Iowa Jima opened their bathing facilities to us, though the attitudes of the 82 Airborne, who had moved onto the ship, made the entire thing uncomfortable (they became hostile if you offered to wash their back). We continued using the water truck.

There was nothing to do. We volunteered at local businesses to sweep up mud and debris. We cleaned a park of broken limbs and downed trees. President Bush flew in and we were set to patrol the Mississippi. To protect him from water borne threats (whatever that meant). Not a boat was in sight. A bulb went out on one of our vessel's running lights and I was the "engineer" so it was my responsibility to fix it. I stole a bulb from a liberty van and spliced it into the wiring system, then duct taped it to the bulkhead. The BM1 said it looked like shit.

A CG officer from Station New Orleans had returned to find his home in Slidell wiped out by high surf. He recruited us to help demolition the sheetrock, in hopes of salvaging the house. During the demolition we watched him dig through his old moldy belongings: photographs, food, linens, furniture, clothing – all trash. He asked us to throw the furniture in the back yard. Elfkin and I were breaking apart his bed when a box of dildos and plugs spilled out onto the floor. We both braced for a joke and the officer stomped over and kicked the rubber toys into a trash bin. His face went flush and he spilt anger into the air. We hurried out of the room with mattress in tow.

A marine retail business was in that neighborhood and a handful of pontoon boats were sitting in plain view, wrapped in chains, secured for the storms. We coerced the owner into letting us use the boats to patrol in the local marinas, harbors and local channels – to patrol the area for looters and perform body recovery. In teams of two we putted around the shoreline of Slidell, gawking at the devastation. My partner, Jacob, was growing depressed from the horrible sights, and my stomach wasn't up for the smells anymore. We moored ourselves to a collapsed bridge and stood sentinel over our small corner of Louisiana. We saw nothing but clouds and debris. No body. Nobody.

A second hurricane was approaching and the Iowa Jima set sail. The Cutter cut lines too, and we were left, again, wondering what to do. The BM1 had found a van and the 15 of us headed for a large Coast Guard base in Mobile. Ten of our team left from there, home to San Francisco. The rest of us were charged with trailering two 25' safe boats back to New Orleans, to relieve a Coast Guard unit protecting an CG ammunitions base. Elfkin and I drove one of the trucks, mesmerized by the feeling of driving through modern ghost towns.

The wind from the second storm shut down the Lake Pontchartrain Bridge and we asked a nearby hotel for refuge. The owner let us sleep in their conference room. We didn't have our overnight gear. The BM1 had us stand a four-hour watch rotation in the hotel conference room. Elfkin and I spent the watch chatting to the hotel owner, a supposed widow who "was looking for some fun." She rolled a joint for us and Elfkin showed her the fun wanted as I stood watch. I sat on the hotel's stoop smoking, staring at the extreme downpour, zapped out of my internal solitude by roaring thunder and nearby lightning bolts.

We made it to the CG munitions facility the next day and found that the 82nd Airborne had sought shelter there and had struck a deal to take over the security of the base. The Sergeant First Class (Army) denied us entry to the Coast Guard Base. And he told us to drive North and report to the air field in Baton Rouge for further orders. The BM1 turned purple and his face locked to his jaw. A group of soldiers could be heard laughing out the window. We turned our Coastie Convoy around and headed North.

We were on a 747 in civilian clothes, jeans and t-shirts, on a flight towards Sacramento. I overheard the couple beside me whispering about how I smelled. I didn't have access to cash, so I couldn't buy drinks on the flight.

Days later my legs broke out in dermatitis and painful fluid sacs developed under my skin around my knees and ankles. The sick-call doctor said I needed to wash my clothes and take showers more often. I started to respond to his uninformed statement, though he shut me down and disclaimed that he was the superior, and I was to follow orders. "Now stay clean out there, as I'm ordering you to do."

YARN 63
ASHORE, PRE-VETERAN

Veterans Day was approaching and the command volunteered two boat crews to participate in the San Jose Veteran's Day Parade. They sought one volunteer, specifically, to "represent the entire Coast Guard as the grand marshal of the event." Before EM3 Hunter completed his tour, he suggested I volunteer for everything, to earn attention and trust from the command, in order to be considered for more prestigious roles and operations. I volunteered.

Decked-out in Dress Blues, freshly pressed, complete with a dozen ribbons[99] on my chest and a flask in my back pocket, the boat crews dropped me off at my designated location. My point of contact, Erica, an obese anxiety filled woman, found me by sight and started giving me the rundown of the day's events. A stretch hummer would carry myself and one member from each of the Armed Forces. Our "float" was the first in the parade. I handed her the personal bio I'd been asked to write, and she quickly read through it. "Were you in Afghanistan or Iraq?".

"Neither."

"Well this float is for Veterans of Foreign Wars."

---

[99] Ribbons: small pieces of fabric little girls and dirty hippies put in their hair. Also, a merit badge for grown men in the military, to be worn on the chest with formal dress, not to be confused with medals, which are said to be "superior" to ribbons (though medals come with ribbons).

A sense of distress started building in my stomach. Calmly and with an annoyed look I said, "I was just told to write a bio and arrive at this location. I wasn't given details."

"Shit. Well it's too late now. Just get in." And she directed me towards the other service members, all of whom just overheard our conversation.

As I walked passed them I reached deep in my pockets to find something to distract my mind, I apologized for the confusion. The limo was stripped of all its food and beverage complements, so I pulled out my flask. At some point we started moving. Erica asked us to stand up and hang out the sun roofs. As we waved to the little kids with giant stuffed animals, wife-beater-wearing guys with obese spouses, and old people in traditional veteran get-ups, the Navy guy started talking to me. "So, why'd you get in if you aren't a war veteran?"

The limo stopped in front of the grand stands. Four bios were read. I stood like a doofus, waving at the people who waved to me, for five pro-longed minutes. Plastic cheers from the plastic crowd. My bio was not read. We started moving. I sat down and pulled out my flask.

The remainder of the parade I watched the waists and legs of four superbly dressed military members. My flask emptied. Erica kept glancing up from her laptop, in my direction, rolling her eyes. Her sigh could be heard each time, above the noise of the party outside.

MK3 POJACK ASHORE, BIO

Enlisted in September 2002, Anchorage Alaska. Born and raised in Goochland Virginia. Petty Officer Pojack Ashore has made multiple deployments on a 378-foot cutter, ranging from drug interdiction in the Sea of Cortez, to immigrant recovery off the Coast of Costa Rica. MK3 Ashore completed at 93-day deployment in the Bering Sea, conducting fishery patrols and joint operations with Russian Ice Breakers. In 2003, Ashore's cutter, the Thrill, was assigned to the Gulf of Alaska to protect the oil refineries, at the onset of the Operation Iraqi Freedom. In 2004 he graduated from Machinery Technician "A" School to become a petty officer 3rd class. As a member of the Maritime Law Enforcement Unit, San Francisco, Ashore is a qualified tactical boat crew member, Boarding Team Member, and is training to become a Military Diver. PO Ashore spent three months in the Hurricane Katrina Recovery effort and was awarded the Humanitarian Medal for his services there.

YARN 64

JON, DC2

Jon had a black CJ-7. The tires were large enough to drive over medians and across ditches without feeling anything. Because Jon and Charles were on sister ships, and their deployments were staggered, Charles had a key to Jon's jeep. The brothers shared most everything.

Charles did not, however, have a key to Jon's house. Jon's roommates forbade it, after Charles drank three of the house's bottles of Jagermeister and shat in a potted plant in the living room. So when Charles arrived in a stupor in the middle afternoon and couldn't get in the house, he just crawled into the back of the CJ and feel asleep in the floorboard, a pile of old uniforms over him to stay warm.

At my place, Jon and I were bored. Rambo, Karen and Red had left earlier to visit the bar at the Oakland Children's Zoo, and Jon and I missed the free ride. At noon, we decided to take Jon's jeep to Shammies.

Jon also had a stool at Shammies, though Alice, the bartender, made him sit in the corner. Jon was allowed to order drinks by placing his empty glass on the bar with cash – but he was not allowed to converse with the bartenders (he had a bad history but was a profitable customer). Around midnight we successfully stole a neon Anchor-Steam sign plus a life-sized cardboard Budweiser cheerleader. We were high-tailing it down the street when Jon stumbled and dropped the sign. The anchor shattered into oblivion. Jon bent down and tried sweeping up the glass dust with his hands, apologizing profusely at the inanimate objects.

"Jon, let's fucking go man. Where's your truck again?" We both knew where it was supposed to be parked, but it wasn't there. We circled the street. Jon's hand bleeding. The Budweiser Girl's arm fell off.

"Somebody stole my jeep, Ashore!"

"Dude. I think you're right. It was right here."

Jon loved his CJ. He pulled out his phone and dialed three numbers without thinking about it. "Yes Hi. My name is Petty Officer Jon Black. I'm in the US Coast Guard. I want to report a auto hijacking.... A. Uh. I mean someone stole my car. My CJ...."

I watched him with a giant smile on my face. Each word made him sound more like a drunk jackass. He was talking to the cops and he was too drunk to get out his message.

"No ma'am... Yes ma'am... Yes I want to report theft. Uh. Auto theft of my CJ-7....uh huh... Yeah but it's gone.. I mean... uh. No. No ma'am... Like two, maybe three... uh. A few hours.... Like noon... Yes I know it's midnight... Uh.... But can you send an officer? I'm at fireside."

"Dude. We're at Shammies."

"Oh I mean Shammies Pub. Not fireside like I just said.... No I'm not drunk.... Hello?... Hello?"

Jon hung up. "You alright?"

"We have to go down there dude. They want me to come in and make a report. They won't send an officer."

"Can we get a beer first?"

W e sat down at the bar. The bartender gave an annoyed look when Jon pulled up a seat. I looked at her, "Hey Alice. Jon's truck was stolen and we're about to go down to the police station. Can he chill here for a sec while we drink a beer?"

"Yeah, I guess. What do you want?"

"A pitcher, please ma'am."

She smiled at me and gently said "coming up." My lips raised slightly, just like my dick, and I put a $2 tip on the counter.

Jon and I discussed the plan. To walk across town, about a mile, and fill out the paper work. We would then walk back to housing and re-evaluate in the morning.

Alice came over, "So, what's happening? Are you sure you boys just didn't leave the car somewhere else? It's probably not a good idea to go to the police station in your condition."

I looked deep into her eyes and kept a soft smile on my face. "Yeah, but we know where we parked, and his truck is gone. It's been stolen, so we have to risk it. I don't think the cops will give us a hard time."

"Uh huh." She grinned and refilled our beers. "Well. If you want a ride, I'm closing shop in 30 minutes. Help me clean up and I'll drive you over there."

As we drove across town, I sat in the middle seat of her little Ford Ranger, Jon resting against the passenger window. My hand ended up on Alice's jeans, above her crotch, and a relationship started that would end my Coast Guard career and ignite my stomach ulcers.

Jon and I were on an adrenaline kick and didn't think about the obvious states of consumption we were operating under. At the dispatcher's window, in the station, Jon spoke up. "Yes. I called in earlier to report my truck being stolen."

"Uh huh. And you want to make that report right now? I would recommend you coming back tomorrow, but if you want I can get an officer for you."

"Yeah we want to report it now."

I started getting cold feet, but Jon seemed to be in control, so I waited.

An officer came into the lobby and eye-balled Jon and I. Jon never got the chance to speak.

"OK you two. Here's what's gonna happen. You will both turn around and walk back to wherever your home is, you can come back in the morning. Or, the second option, we can find you a room in the holding tank, while I call your base and let them know you're here."

Jon started to speak but was cut off.

"Look. I'm not going to have a discussion. It is either the holding cell, right now, or home. You pick in three seconds. One..."

I turned and walked out. Jon was behind me.

It took an hour to walk the two miles back to Jon's house. We complained the entire way as our alcohol slowly burnt off and left us in pain, too late at night to purchase more. At the 7/11 we bought old hot dogs and Gatorade. By the time we arrive to Jon's we were exhausted and he said I could sleep on his couch. We almost walked right by his jeep without realizing the significance of it.

"Holy shit Jon! How the fuck!"

"What the fuck!" Jon ran to the jeep to inspect. "Dude it's here. How did it get here?" He jumped in the driver seat and looked at the ignition. Then he looked in the back seat. A pile of shit on the floor board. "What the fuck?" He pulled away some old clothes.

Charles was lying in a ball on the floor. Unconscious and unaware he'd just been exposed by his older brother. "Charles! Wake the fuck up!" Jon screamed.

"I'm up. I'm up... Oh hey Jon. What's going on?"

"Charles what the fuck are you doing. Did you take my car?"

Charles looked confused and half asleep. Wedged between the front and rear seats, he un-pretzeled himself as he told his story. "Dude. It was the craziest thing. I've slept walked before, but I never slept drove. I was sleeping here earlier this morning and I drove the car to Shammies in my sleep. Haha. No shit. I woke up over by Shammies a few hours ago. So I just drove her back. Where've you been all day?" He looked in my direction. "Sup Ashore?"

YARN 65

POND, BM2

E ach Dive Team member had to give approval before they would grant me final permission to attend dive school. Pond was the last to sign off on me, and he took me for one last work out.

"Run those fucking demons out, Ashore." Mile 8 and he was having me sprint. My calves were dry from a dehydration, but I pushed on to his commands. "Stop. Get Down, Get Down, Get Down... Get Up. Get Down. Get Up. Get Down. Ready! Push-ups! Beeeggin!

"1.2.3.1. 1.2.3.2. 1.2.3.3. 1.2.3.4.................1.2.3.20...

"Is that all you got you fucker? You think you can get through dive school? You're gonna drop out in the first day if you show weakness like this shit. Get the fuck up. Get down. Up! Let's go. Keep up with me."

I followed Pond 10 miles that day and we did over 100 push-ups, sit-ups and flutter kicks. When we turned back towards base we were two miles away and he picked up his pace, "you better beat me back, Ashore. Everyone is waiting and you better get there first or you're out."

Pond was a machine. If he wanted to, he could have skipped at a faster pace than me, non-stop. I wasn't used to long distance, specifically not 10 miles. My asshole was burning. My nipples were burning. My calves were tight.

I had extended my contract with the guard by a year and had trained 6 months to get signed off to go to dive school, so I did what anyone would do. I forced my body to shut up, I put my lungs into overdrive, and started sprinting. Pond was right beside me. "That's all you got? That's it?" I could hear him panting and his strides adjusted. Some sort of second or third wind came over me, and I felt a relief of pain and a fresh dose of exhilaration. I widened my pace. I could see the Coast Guard Base's bridge and I picked up my speed even more. I could barely breathe. Mr. S. was by the security gate and waved us through. Pond was cheering at this point: "Go! Go! Go! Go!." I rounded the last corner and there were the four other members of the dive team, and about ten other guys form the unit chanting. "Ashore! Ashore! Ashore! Ashore!." I sprinted directly past the parking lot and collapsed in the grass. *I made it. I fucking made it!* I laid heaving, my chest about to burst. Mr. S. jogged up behind me with an envelope. "Your orders are in here Ashore, I'll throw them on your locker. Good Job."

That night, full of energy and adrenaline, I went home to my new girlfriend's place, Alice's. We had been seeing each other on and off for a few weeks, and had committed to loose monogamy. At her house we opened a bottle of tequila and I started switch hitting: shot, beers, shot, beer... I felt untouchable! I had quit smoking a few months before, though I decided I could have one in celebration. I stepped onto her front porch and lit the cigarette. I was pacing back and forth, day dreaming, when my right foot slipped off the porch ledge and slid a few steps. I caught myself on the railing. The top of my right foot was in pain instantly. I didn't know it but a stress fracture spread across the arch of my foot.

Three weeks later in the middle of Dive School, I reported to the sick-call with an unbearable amount of pain in my foot. After X-Rays they would tell me I could go on medical leave, and probably never become a diver, or I could suck it up. Sucking it up cost me a permanent limp and the pains that spread from that.

YARN 66

ETNF3 GOBY, DIVER

The Navy guys were all small. Averaging 5.5' at 140lbs. Cut. Trim. Hilarious. Moving around the showers amongst these sailors was dangerous. They didn't talk much about work life. All submariners, they were at dive school for reasons they wouldn't discuss (classified I assumed). They had no issues with physical touch, slaps, play. The motto of the day was always "it's not gay if the balls don't touch."

We'd wake up and run. Do some push-ups. Run. Sit-ups. Run. Pull-ups. Run. Indian runs. Cadence calling, "Let 'em kill, let 'em kill. Let the Marine Corps kill. From the East to the West. US Marine Corps is the best."

More running. Swimming, hands aren't allowed to break the surface. Breath holds. Fist in the gut. Instructor on top of you, holding you down. Feel comfortable and relax as things get dark. Bubbles. Then air. Breathe. Yells in your direction. Push-ups. "Get up, Get up, Get up! Get down. Ready! Begin: 1. 2. 3. 1. 1. 2. 3. 2. 1. 2. 3. 3." Etc...

Coax Goby into heading to the bars after our evening class. Spring in Panama City. Drunk would happen fast. Bodies craving calories and sleep. Wake up. Run. Sit ups. Push-ups. Vomit in shirt. Slime slides down belly, into tighty-whities, out of the bottom of

UDTs[100], down running legs. Chunks of French-fries and stomach vile. "Let 'em dig, let em' dig. Let the Army Dig..."

"Ashore! What the fuck does the Coast Guard need divers for Ashore? You guys ever go into water above your waist?" Goby was our cadence caller, and he'd bust my balls every chance he could.

"Alright, people. Nuts to butts. Nuts to butts. You have five minutes to take your shower and be at your desk. I wanted to see skin thirty seconds ago. Let's do this. Go! Go! Go!."

"Who wants to go to the bar with me tonight? Goby? I'm buying."

---

[100] UDTs: Hot shorts. Originally worn by Naval Underwater Demolition Teams, they are now worn by many military units that have standard physical exercise regiments.

YARN 67

ASHORE, DIVER

*The Diana's crew – a set of worthless outcasts who
had been picked up at the islands from the refuse
of whale-ships...*
—*Richard Henry Dana Jr.*

My first adventurous deployment as a diver was a joint Op with the dive team from my MLEU and the dive team from Seattle's MLEU. The orders said to meet in Kodiak, and board the Buoy Tender Sprit, to recover buoys which had drifted from station during the recent storms (This is not true, the buoys held station. The channel itself moved). The deployment was to take between 30 and 60 days. My excitement was through the roof, though I was a bit nervous of what Alice would say, as I had just returned from Florida's dive school weeks before.

My flight for Kodiak was two days out, so I didn't waste time telling Alice. When we sat down that evening, I surprised her with flowers and tickets to a Dead show for that summer. She seemed hesitant to accept my offers. There was tension in the air, and I suspected she could see me holding back what I really needed to say. I took a long drink and reached for her hands across the table. When I told her about my orders she responded with quick anger. Caught off guard I stood up to leave. "No wait. Don't go," she pleaded. Then she showed me a positive pregnancy test.

I n Kodiak my mind was full. We were training daily and prepping our gear for below freezing water temps. Shadowing my team, I offered no meaningful feedback, nothing social. I knew I was proving to be a disappointment to my Dive Officer – my enthusiastic demeanor had changed. He didn't know why.

The day before the Sprit was scheduled to get underway, the dive teams went out for a round at the local bar. The team from Seattle had younger guys on it, and when they pushed me to get excited about 'being Divers,' the whole bravado "OORAH!" thing, I left the group and headed off on my own.

At Bernie's Bar, on some back street, in the dark of the night, I was on the verge of a major drunk when I decided to head back to the hotel. As I walked down the street, a cop drove by and shined a light in my face. Before I knew it, I was in the back of his car. Without any discussion I was pushed into a holding cell, apparently for being drunk in public, though I didn't feel that I had done anything wrong. With concern about missing movement, and frigid temperatures in the cell, I huddled in a corner as a horrible realization set in. *Fucking Cops.*

About an hour after arriving, a second man was thrown into the cell beside me. Soon, two officers appeared, one claimed to be "The Sherriff." He said there had been a mistake and I was picked up as "meeting the description of a vandal in the area" – the guy who was just thrown in the cell beside me. When I said I had to catch a Coast Guard ship within a few hours, the Sherriff apologized profusely and said he'd drive me to my hotel. On the way he reminded me that I was obviously intoxicated and the police had a right to keep me regardless. I made it to the hotel at 0300.

At that point in my career I had never been late, and never received a negative write-up. The following morning, I awoke to a phone call. I was late to muster by 30 minutes. I was out the door, no shower, no shave, smelling like ass, in 5 minutes. We walked on the boat as a team, late, because of me.

We set sail for the Aleutian Islands, a massive hangover in tow. As the lowest ranking member on the team I berthed with the ship's non-rates and lower level petty officers. During dive school I quit smoking, but I was back to it. From the rails of the Sprit's fantail, I leaned, stared, and blew smoke through the falling snow. The shoreline was always within sight, it drifted by, our heavy steel hull rolling 10 degrees back and forth. The mountains of Alaska. Little huts with chimneys puffing. Ice floats. Trawling boats in the distance.

YARN 68

BM3 SLY

S ly met us at Oakland International Airport. He parked in front of the baggage claim in the GV, flipped on the blue lights, and strolled inside like he owned the place. The Chief frowned but didn't say anything. I felt the first smile on my face since leaving for Alaska a month before.

Sly started shaking our hands a welcoming us back. He was a genuinely nice guy, he wanted to know about our adventures. The Chief and the GM1 said they were anxious to see their families so they assigned Sly and myself to wait for the baggage and to get it safely stowed back on base. They left for the taxi platform.

"Dude how was it?"

"It was good man. Alaska always seems to calm me. It's hard to find any sense of peace in the world, and Alaska does that to me."

"What's up man? You seem off." Sly called my bluff.

"Shit dude. I'm carrying a heavy load, brother. The Dive Chief is pissed because my head's been in my ass the entire trip... Fucking Alice is pregnant."

"The bartender?"He started laughing.

"I think I need to marry her. At least the BAH will make things easier."

The baggage conveyor warning light and buzzer alarmed and the conveyor started moving.

"Dude. Slow down brother. I don't know the details or anything, but it sounds like you're trying to rush into something."

"My head's a wreck. What the fuck do I do? I know she's panicking. She would hardly talks to me on the phone."

"Look man. I went through something similar before I failed out of college. Everything worked itself out, and I never had to talk to the chick again. Haha. I think you just got to slow down man."

An emotional urge flushed over me and I couldn't fight it off. "I gotta go smoke real quick."

H eading back to base I was lost in thought. I knew Alice was going to be working so I anticipated going to Shammies. Despite Sly's words of wisdom, I'd made up my mind to ask Alice to marry me. The BAH level would bring over $2000 to my base pay and that provided comfort would, in theory, help our relationship.

"So what do you think about Olympia?"

I looked over at Sly cautiously. "What about it?"

"Well, they're saying it could take weeks or months. That the Dive team will be the first ones to leave."

My heart skipped a beat. "Wait! What the fuck are you talking about?"

"The Olympia trip next week. The Dive team is leaving with the armory this weekend. I saw your name on the list bro."

"Olympia, Washinton? What the Fuck! When did this happen?"

"They told us a few days ago. Apparently they are expecting major protest and they want an entire MLEU on location.

YARN 69

BM1 O'BRIEN

Olympia only lasted two weeks, plus a two day convoy on either side. Mr. S.' face went blank when I told him I had a shotgun marriage before we left. On the deployment, volunteers were asked to leave early and I was the first to pipe up. Mr. S. said I'd committed to being a diver and I was obliged to do just that. "You can volunteer to hump a piling[101]. You cannot volunteer to leave early."

Back in the Bay I was assigned once again with the Boat Crews. O'Brien's comment brought me out of a day-dream. "Fucking wharf-rats[102] in Richardson's Bay. We need to send a 378 through here at speed; send a wake to sink all these fuckers. Look at that one. Oh, shit. That fucking thing is a floating shed, straight out of that movie. Fuck. What is that movie called? Oh, yeah. 'Deliverance.' Fucking hillbilly cabin floating right here in our back yard."

---

[101] Hump Piling: A diver wraps arms and legs around a piling and moves up and down it. This would effectively find am IED if one were attached to the said piling.

[102] Wharf Rat: see Jerry Garcia's sketch "August West." (Dead)

Shivers: "O'Brien, you think these guys are cooking meth or what?" Shivers, again with a stupid comment. I always got stuck between the asshole and the twat.

O'Brien: "Nah. These fuckers just sit around rocking on their modified front porches wearing their 'Who Farted?' wife-beaters. They aren't smart enough to cook meth. Ashore, what'd you think? Should we wake 'em out?"

Me: "Man, leave the fuckers alone. They're just trying to get by like everyone else."

O'Brien: "Get by my ass, Ashore? They're fucking free loaders. Look at these shit holes. You think they have sanitation systems in these shacks. Fuck no. They just hang their ass right over the side and shit. Next time you go diving think about that – shit floating next to your face mask."

Shivers: "Hey look at this person. What's she smoking?"

O'Brien: "Shit. She's looking this way."

O'Brien leaned his head out the window. "Howdy Ma'am. Just cruising around on a lovely day." He tipped his hat to her.

YARN 70

BM3 ROSSI

When I arrived to the unit, Rossi had had his coxswain certification pulled because he was jumping the waves under the Golden Gate Bridge, to the point where the entire hull and props would come out of the water. The command had just given his cert back and I was put on his boat crew for a special deployment into the Sacramento Delta. An area of the world known for rednecks, meth, and fishing. It takes about an hour to get there going 30 knots by boat. We were going to patrol a specific area where massive populations of drunk boaters tie up and anchor for the Fourth of July weekend party.

When we arrived on scene, we were completely caught off guard. There were thousands of small water craft anchored, moored and grounded in one small lagoon that had waters less than 4' deep. Our objective was to show presence and it was decided we would take our two boats straight through the middle of the crowd – we were the only law enforcement there and a majority of the rednecks had never heard of the Coast Guard, much less knew what our jurisdiction or authority was.

Because of the nature of the crowds, the Boarding Officers had a crew member man the M240 on the bow on the boat, not because we needed it, but to protect it in case some drunk jumped onto our boat. I was volunteered for the job. As we entered the dense group of boaters, drunks and swimmers, it quickly became apparent that we were not wanted there. Heckles, boos and jeers came from the crowds. I did everything I could to keep my chin up and not acknowledge the torments. We reached a place where there was no option but to let our bow rest, and then push, other boats out of our way – something we've been trained not to do. At that moment a group of bikini clad girls on a jet ski started yelling at me. "Hey cowboy, nice big gun you got there! Hehe. You compensating for something?" I looked down to avoid eye contact. "Aw, you sad now. You gonna cry." I pulled myself together and looked in their direction and gave a half-assed awkward smile. They started laughing profusely. More jeers from the opposite side of the boat, and I decided to turn that way. I then found a comfortable way to lean on the M240. *So embarrassing.*

Over the next 30 minutes Rossi got the boat through the crowd. He pushed the throttles open all the way home. No one talked for the 60 minute trip. As we putted into the Coast Guard base Rossi broke the silence: "Has anyone heard the rumors of another San Diego deployment?"

YARN 71

ALICE, BARTENDER

I was carrying a beautiful alcoholic conflagration
around with me.
—Jack London

She was soaked in sweat as she rode his dick harder and harder. She clawed at his chest. He held her hips and thrusted upwards each time she pounced down. Up and down, up and down. Her breasts were small enough to not to hurt her as she bounced, but they were present enough for the stranger to reach up and grab them every so often. She couldn't help but be distracted by the fact she was fucking on the pool table again. "It's better to be on top. I hate bending over this gross table," she thought. She clawed harder at his chest; more to cover up the anchor-and-shield tattoo than to feel his solid pecs. Her vagina felt fantastically full. In a few moments, she knew, she'd have to find another distraction. The bar was closed. She could drink herself away.

Her thoughts were so deep she didn't sense the signs the stranger was about to cum and he let loose inside of her. "God damnit!"

"Oh Sorry. Are you on the pill or something?"

Alice jumped off. "You don't just fucking cum in somebody dude." She stormed behind the bar naked and grabbed a bar-rag. An awkward silence followed.

"You want a shot?" she said as she cleaned herself.

The guy fumbled for his pants and shirts. Grabbed his shoes and sat across the bar from Alice. "I'm sorry about blowing inside you. I just thought—"

"I can't get pregnant. Don't worry. I just don't want some stranger Coastie's cum inside me." She paused and shook away her thoughts. "Whatever. Are you drinking or not?"

"Yeah I'll drink. How'd you know I was in the Coast Guard?"

"You have the fucking tattoo. Jesus." She pulled out a bottle of rail-liquor and poured two full glasses. Slid one across the bar. Took a giant swig from hers. "Everybody is a fucking Coastie in this fucking town."

She started acting like she truly felt and the stranger was a bit confused, so he drank faster. "Well, I guess that's true. But you're not a Coastie."

"Yeah, well I'm married to one," she almost laughed, or cried. She took another pull from her drink, leaving the glass mostly empty. As she refilled it she blurted out, "And I'm fucking pregnant by one too."

She couldn't stop the tears. Her naked body suddenly felt the immense cold around her and she squatted into the modified fetal position and started balling. Her glass still in hand. The motion of her squat forced jiz to drip out of her, but she didn't notice it.
The stranger looked left and right, and thought really hard about his obligations. He put his shoes on and slammed the rest of his cheap whiskey. "Well it was nice meeting you. Maybe I should—"

"Just fucking go. Everyone just fucking leaves. Fuck me. Leave me. I don't give a shit." She stood up fast and pointed a hard finger at the door. "Just fucking go!"

"Ok, Ok. I'm sorry. I just didn't know what to do. I'm leaving."

She bent over the bar and started crying harder. He walked towards the door. Looked at the clock behind the bar and subconsciously subtracted 15 minutes. Felt a horrible sense of guilt. He turned back and took a step towards Alice. "Look. I'm sorry about tonight. I can give you a ride home if you need it. Can I do anything for you?"

"Nobody can do anything for me."

That was the sentence the stranger didn't want to hear. His guilt forced him into the role of a fucking therapist for some emotionally savaged bartender. He walked back to his bar stool (which was actually my barstool, but I was in San Diego at this point) and sat, leaned over the counter, and placed a hand on Alice's back. "If you need a ear, I've got two."

ALICE UNLEASHES ON STRANGER

"My dad was an overweight cornhusker that drank too much. I couldn't take it. My twin sister and I ran away for her boyfriend's house in Lincoln. We hitched a ride with a trucker on Highway 80. I'll never forget it. Jesus. He said he'd take us as far as we wanted to go, even to San Francisco, if we made it worthwhile. In the four days it took us to make it here. It was so gross. In the city, he stopped in the Haight to buy speed. That's when we met Alan. Alan was a kid on the Haight that took me and Sarah under his wing, that's my sister's name – Sarah. He was cool. He taught us the ropes. Where we could pitch a tent. How to use YMCA for their free showers. How to score cheap weed and how to sell it. Within a few months Sarah and I had a name for ourselves. We ran the Masonic Corner, right outside of the brewery Magnolia, you know the one? Anyways, we sold weed during the day, got fucked up at night, and either crashed in the park or made our way to the dirty Scumbard motels – you know the ones? Anyways. We did that for years it seems like. We were 16 when we arrived on the Haight. I was arrested a few times. Haha. It was crazy. Ten times better than being around my ass-slapping dad. Fuck the system, man. It's all fucked. Then Sarah met some dude that got her hooked on meth. Just like them all, they start slow and laugh about it. She started selling the shit. Did a few week's in Bryant St. They only let her go because of her age. She was hooked on it. Got pregnant twice. During her second pregnancy I told her we were getting out of there. I landed a job here and we moved into the slums in Oakland. Over on Mead? You know? Have you heard of it? Anyways. She can't get clean. Her kids are with my mom now. I was always the good one. Always. I never touch that hard shit. Well I dabble at shows, but who doesn't? Right? Sarah started using needles a few months ago and I kicked her and her zitty boyfriend out. Fucking gross people man. Right? And that's about the time I met Pojack and I thought—

The stranger jerked awake! "Wait.... What!?! Ashore?"

Alice's story came to an abrupt halt. They both realized their situation instantaneously. "Hey. I really think I should go now." He finished his drink again, unbolted the door, and walked out without looking back. Through the frost-glass window she could see his silhouette quickly walk by.

She stood stiff, frozen, still naked, for a long moment. Then started crying as she refilled her glass.

JOURNAL ENTRY

(June 2006) Alice and I don't seem to be doing well. They gave us a housing unit in Novato instead of BAH. Haha. Never saw that coming... I went out with a few of the reservist last night. Against my rules, I know, but I needed the company. A theatre in the city commemorating the hippie movement was calling. We brought a bottle of Jack with us. I remember stealing a bicycle. Hiding from a flashlight. Laughing. Yelling. Running. Running. Transiting an alley way. In the O-Town. Running around. Bad was funny. I gave a crack head my money... When I awoke in my truck, my phone was ringing. I looked at it and saw a dozen missed calls. I was late to work by hours. I had missed movement. Fuck.

(July 2006) The Mast went well. Going in I was nervous, though there is something about a uniform that helps manage that. I look good in a uniform, I wear it well.

I walked in the room, body stiff and everything about me mechanical. The little conference room was flooded with officers and petty officers, many who were there as part of their signoffs for promotions. The Captain came in, a list of my charges read, and the Captain said, "Ashore, you've helped this team tremendously. You have no negative write-ups in your file. All of your superiors vouch for you. If I see you again, I'll take your Dive Pin. Dismissed."

That was it. It took less than two minutes in total and I was outside. I quickly got in my truck and smoked half a pack of cigarettes as I drove to Shammie Dammies to celebrate! I got sloshed and now my dress-blues are covered in bar juice.

YARN 72
RAMBO, KAREN AND RED

"You look like shit Ashore."

"Yeah well, Some People Like Their Cucumbers Pickled."

"I don't think it's funny. Red, tell him he looks like shit."

"You like shit dude."

I raised my hand in the air and snapped. The waitress looked in our direction. "Una Mas!" She was probably going to spit in my drink, but I didn't care.

"What's everyone up to over the Holidays?"

"We're going to the Tahoe 'A' Frames again! Rambo's going, aren't you Rambo?"

"Fuck yeah, I'm going. Ashore, you want to join us? But you can't bring your dog. Uh, I mean bitch."

Karen jumped on him for being an asshole, but I expected it. Alice was being a bitch. "I can't go. They are sending me to a fucking thing in San Diego again."

"You fucked yourself man. I told you not to volunteer for shit."

"Yeah, well I stopped volunteering when I got back from Florida."

A waiter came over to our table and put a beer down. He paused and we all looked at him. "Hey guys. We know you come here a lot, and we appreciated your business. But we're going to have to cut off your friend here after this round." He looked at everyone but me, then walked away.

"What the fuck did I do?"

"Dude. You're fine. They're just being assholes. Let's go to Shammies. Or, no, let's go to the fucking Moon Tree!"

Karen jumped at Rambo. "He's not fine. Tell him he's fine and he's going to think he's fine. Ashore, you're a ship-wreck. You look like shit. You smell like shit. You can't make it through a sentence without slurring or yelling at someone. What the fuck happened to you?"

I stood up and looked in my wallet. *No cash.* "Fuck this." I walked out and headed downhill.

YARN 73
ASHORE, PETTY OFFICER

After Kodiak, and between deployments, I was back on normal work detail. Alice was emotional, pregnant, and worried, and getting married seemed a thing to do, and marriage was supposed to come with more money in the form of BAH. A month after our Court-House wedding we were denied BAH and assigned a Coast Guard housing unit. I was given temporary assignments to Seattle, followed by San Diego, Concord, and San Diego again. At some point between those deployments, Alice decided to abort and hide the procedure from me as a miscarriage. I missed movement and was masted. I began to suspect Alice was cheating. Our phone conversations were never pleasant. The short stays at home, between deployments were full of fights and accusations. Our marriage from months earlier was finished before it really started.

I had extended my contract by a year to go to dive school. Not only that, I had given my word to my command that I wanted to do more, to participate and help the unit grow. Each night, away and home, I'd find escape at dark bars and there I'd consolidate my dissonance by drinking. After arriving home from a deployment early, to surprise Alice on Christmas morning. I found her in our bedroom with some guy, his IHOP waiter uniform on the floor in the living room. I walked out of the house, found a liquor store, bought two jugs of wine and proceeded to drink.

My contract with the guard flooded with booze, quick. Sinking. *Sinking. Sinking.*

U nder power-lines in the rain, sitting in mud, looking at San Pablo Bay. *Wish I had a boat.* My focus was a disaster. I used every ounce of strength to block my thought process. Alice was still at home, guy there too. In my truck, I dumped my wine into an old 7/11 cup. Headed for the Coast Guard base, to sleep. I had duty the next day – *I can sleep under a desk.*

As I approached the CG security gate, I fumbled my strategy. *Better not drive on base drunk.* Headed for Lucky's. Played pool and ordered shots of vodka mixed straight with V8 – something I do whenever my stomach ulcers flare up. From a bar-stool perch I could see my reflection through the bottles of Jack behind the bar. An angelic figure beside me in the mirror. Arms around my torso, an offer of love. The bar floor approached my face too quickly to dodge it. Anger in the air. Movement. Things happening.

Dizziness and confusion were coming at me like physical objects. *Did I eat acid?* I climbed towards a flashing light to escape. My back was in fiery pain. A demon with dreadlocks grabbed at me through a fence. In defense I bit and tore at its horns. *Cops.* I heard myself telling an officer I was going to fuck his mother. Scuffling. Screaming and howling. *I gotta get out of here.* "Call my wife! Call my wife!" Blows to my chest. Pain in my wrist. Kicking. An inferno snaking up my spine. I tried to bend backwards to take the pain away. Back about to snap like a twig. *Swaying.* Fainting. Fainting. Falling into darkness. Bobbing up and down, like a cork hitting the crest of a backless wave, climaxing, a sudden descent into a bottomless black trough.

I woke in an isolation chamber in Santa Rita Jail, where I lived for seven days. No communication from either side of my wall. On the last day a guard led me to a concrete room with a small plexiglass window with a hole in it. Mr. S. was on the other side. "What do you have to say for yourself, Ashore?"

"Sir, I don't know what I did sir."

The comprehensive Coast Guard report in the folder on your desk knows what I did. It states I had broken into a warehouse; fell 30 feet onto a slab of concrete; bit a bar patron who tried to help me; called 911 on myself; was arrested for being drunk in public; kicked out a police-car door; jumped on a cop's back and choked him; was tazed by that cop's partner; and was taken to Santa Rita Prison. On the way to Santa Rita I went on a rambling rant about fucking the wives and mothers of my arresting officers so they decided to beat the shit out of me in the parking lot of the prison.

After seven days, my Coast Guard unit took responsibility of me and the county let me go on parole. My private lawyer wanted to sue the city police because I called 911 asking for help (there is a recording of this) and instead I wound up tazed, soaked in purple and black skin and cuff rash. And though my lawyer said we could win a lot of money, I struck a deal between all parties, to have all charges dropped, on both sides. Four months later I was in the civilian sector again, with no wife and no dog, my tail between my legs, and a hunkering to go to sea once more.

I had become a sailor...
I was Jacked.

JOURNAL ENTRY

(February 2007) My second mast. More sharp uniforms and ribbons. He took my dive pin as he said he would. Not that it matters. He put me in line to be discharged. Guess he could have given me the brig. I'm not sure I care anymore. They have me going to rehab next week. I suspect Alice will disappear by then.

I fucked a fat girl last night and wrote a song about it:

I've been drinkin my whiskey
With every mornin cup of Joe[103].
Stayin drunk a dirty
Listenin to David Allan Coe.
And I been smokin non-filtered
Drinkin the bar dry
Hidin in dark alcoves
When I need to get high
But I'm scared of the silence
When you can hear yourself sigh
On the walls I write I don't miss you
But I know it's a lie.

---

[103] Cup of Joe: aka coffee. The name is given from the Secretary of Navy, when he banned alcohol aboard Naval ships in 1913. Josephus Daniels. When sailors began complaining, Joe said to drink coffee instead.

SHIPMATES

So I think I'll go and fuck me a fat girl.
Maybe a whore or two.
Anything to ease this pain,
To stop thinking about you

Well you left in such a hurry
Where you went I know
It's been tearing at my heart
Already punctured my soul.
You know what I'm missing.
You know it's not fear
Haven't had a real woman
In nearly a year.
So I think I'll go and fuck me a fat girl.
Maybe a whore or two.
Anything to ease this pain,
To stop thinking about you

MR. S.

Out of rehab, I had another week in the Guard before my discharge was complete. My command restricted me to base and I was living back in The Barracks, which I had lived in when I first arrived to San Francisco. One morning, I was walking down the side walk, in uniform, and I passed by Mr. S., who had left our unit months before, before my destructive episode. I saluted and said "Hey sir."

"Ashore, I wanted to talk to you..."

I cut him off, "Sir I'm sorry for what I did..."

He cut me off, "I don't give a fuck what you did." It was the first time I'd seen him emotional. He was mad at me. Disappointed. "I'm missing my dive watch. I last saw it in the gear box after our Seattle dive. Would you happen to have it?"

By the look on his face I could tell he lacked all faith in me. His assumption was that I stole his watch. I was taken aback[104], I hadn't given him any reason to assume I was a thief.

"No, sir. I haven't seen it, but I can look for you."

"Don't. If it pops up, you can leave it at the front desk in Building 11 for me."

---

[104] Taken Aback – when your sails are pushed backwards, so they rest against which ever mast or spar hold them.

SHIPMATES

PART FOUR

Wrack on the Beach

Bill – John Masefield

He lay dead on the cluttered deck
and stared at the cold skies,
With never a friend to mourn for him
nor a hand to close his eyes:
"Bill, he's dead," was all they said;
"he's dead, 'n' there he lies."

The mate came forrard at seven bell
and spat across the rail:
"Just lash him up wi' some holystone
in a clout o' rotten sail,
'N', rot ye, get a gait on ye,
ye're slower 'n' a bloody snail!"

When the rising moon was a copper disk
and the sea was a strip of steel,
We dumped him down to the swaying weeds
ten fathom beneath the keel.
"It's rough about Bill," the fo'c's'le said,
"we'll have to stand his wheel." (Maesfield, 1902)

YARN 74
BLUEJAY, MERCHANT

When I left the Guard, I was socially worn and beaten. My Captain had given me the option to be reduced in grade to E1 and take a 12-month restriction to base, or to leave under honorable conditions. It wasn't what I wanted; I carried a sense of pride for my beloved service, but, like a majority of my messmates[105], I left the Coast Guard with my tail between my legs, after nearly five years of service. 28 days in a drug and alcohol rehab program were my last days on active duty.

Rehab was an obstacle to spending money, and thanks to that, when I left the Guard, I had few thousand bucks to play with. Half went to my wife so she could drive to Florida and fuck her ex. Tears fell when she said she was taking the dog. The other half paid for travels across the country, first touring with David Allan Coe, mixing mushrooms and Country Western.

Eventually I awoke on Bluejay's porch, in Kittery Bay. On his couch I watched my toes wiggle for months, as I spent hundreds of dollars on Oxycontins[106]. It was in that shape of euphoria that I met Ebony,

---

[105] Messmates: A shipmate who you have eaten with aboard. Traditionally a person who is more intimate than just a shipmate. A close friend aboard your vessel.
[106] Oxycontins: a brand name for Oxycodone. Bliss in pill form.

Bluejay's wife, and their only daughter at that time, Sunshine. The three of them lived in a beautiful cabin by the bay with a huge back yard. We could watch sailboats gracefully move North and South, East over the horizon, their silhouettes at night, quiet, some with loose jibs[107] flapping, reefed[108] mains, in 10 knot breezes. They had another guy living at their house, named Crunchy. Crunchy walked around in a one-piece tie-dyed pajama for my entire stay. When I left Kittery, I was hungry for opiates and had just started my first line of credit – which would last for six months. Bluejay was a happy pot-smoking Coastie and was considering reenlisting after his four-year mark, which he soon did despite my pushing for him to get out.

Two years later, Bluejay had a second child. Then, right on cue, he was booted from the Coast Guard for popping positive on a uranalysis. After five years in the service, he lost everything he worked towards. Though, thankfully, he left with a resume that helped him land a gig in the Merchant Marines.

As a cook for the sailor's union, Bluejay transferred from one ship to another. He was often on ships months at a time, then he'd return home and burn his money. In foreign ports, he'd call, brag about the cleanliness of the cocaine and prostitutes. More pain, listening to adventures and exotic escapades over the ocean; I'd get jealous. Stuck in San Francisco, I had fathered a child within a year of leaving the Guard, who desperately needed me to be home (pardon my digression, though this child's mother was named Dev, not the bar-

---

[107] Jib: forward sail
[108] Reefed: tucking a fabric away. Sails can be reefed to a specific degree, to reduce sail surface or slow down. A shirt can be reef tucked into pants.

tender Alice). I stayed, inland and near coastal, working locally on whatever boats would have me, mostly ferries. Bydrman's stories were more jacked than mine – seaward.

I was lying in bed dreaming about a peaceful night of sleep when Ebony called in panic. She yelled through the phone, desperately upset – Bluejay was in jail in Panama. I knew Bluejay had gotten a job on a tug and barge and was pulling three-months-on-three-months-off rotations. He had expressed his knowledge of the party scene in Panama City, "intense," and he was often hanging out with his Captain doing blow on watch. He said his ATB[109] was semi-permanently moored in a ghetto part of town. When Ebony said he was in jail, I wasn't surprised. When she said that he had called her from the jail and confessed to spending their life savings on cocaine and hookers, I still wasn't surprised, but I felt a little bad for him and for her.

Anchors fouled[110] as yarns unraveled and accumulated on the deck over the following week. Turned out that Bluejay did indeed spend all of his pay on drugs and sex. After being tossed in a jail for possession, he called his wife during his come-down and left a message on her voice mail declaring his drug use and infidelity. By no means in his right mind, his strategy of confession ended up

---

[109] ATB: Articulated tug and barge, where the tug is fastened semi-permanently to the barge via mechanical means.

[110] The fouled anchor is a symbol of trial and suffering at sea. It is worn by chiefs in both the US Navy and US Coast Guard. Before the advent of motors, sailing vessels were dependent on their anchors to prevent unwanted drift, like onto a reef or into breaking waves. A fouled anchor would have to be cut, unless the deck crew were savvy enough to get it back in. Cutting an anchor could mean havoc in the future.

costing him his family, house and bank account. Though in those early weeks, he simply had to focus and get out of jail.

He missed movement. His second time, and his last, since joining the union. Not only his job but his Merchant Mariner Credentials were gone instantly. His elderly father sent bond money, in the realm of $5000, and Bluejay was free long enough to run over the border and turn himself in at a consulate in Honduras. The story he gave the consulate didn't make much sense, but Bluejay was suffering from obvious signs of malnourishment and other illnesses, so the consulate flew him home on the US tax payers' dime, and Bluejay managed to avoid a lengthy prison sentence in the third world.

.

JOURNAL ENTRY

(September 2010)
No more first or last chance at this saloon/I'll take your
dollar down for myself. And if your ghost comes
stumbling round/I'll put it back on the shelf.

There's been a fleet of days in the harbour/ The old
Bay is soaked with rain. This Coastie's been drinking
on Sundays/ the Sailors been drinking like Spring.

Come 'round you hobos and hookers/I've seen your
anchor tattoos! If you'd mourn my friend with me/I'll
buy ya a round or two.

Oh, I'll go to sea a singing/I'll go to sea with glee.
I'll go to sea this evening/ mourning with dirty sailor
company!

YARN 75

NEILSON, CG VET

S hipmates they come, shipmates they go. Some of us leave the Guard with our sea-legs under us. Ready to conquer, excited. The maritime world is small and I stumble onto Coasties and ex-Coasties often. Neilson left the guard with Other Than Honorable conditions, and enrolled directly in the prestigious California Maritime Academy. But he was missing something. Wit? Courage? Social skills? Skills?

I t can take years, decades even, for romantic and/or intimate couples to open themselves to each other. On a ship's bridge, in the sea of night, on watch, the same release happens with near strangers in a tiny fraction of the time. Pilot House confessions are an important cultural piece of the maritime industry.

Neilson and I met in Anacortes, working on delivery boats. Yarning for life. After working isolated with him for almost a year, he unleashed his mind on me. His most shameful, debilitating truth came spilling out. Behavior can be predicted through a number of variables (Genes, Culture, Birth Location, IQ, EQ, Family Social Status, Economic Status, Education levels, Hormones, Number of Years Served in the Coast Guard, Type of Discharge). Yarns can help us predict.

NEILSON'S PILOT HOUSE CONFESSION:

'There is no greater drive of a man than his sex drive.'

I had to explain this to my wife of four years after I cheated on her and was caught.

'You see,' I told her, 'all the guys do it. You've heard of the bars outside of the academy, where the wives hang out when the guys are underway? Well it's true. Women do it too.'

I didn't do it though, Ashore. I never cheated on her. Well, except that one time, but it's not like I fucked anyone. HaHa

I've always been awkward. Katie was only the second women I ever made it with. The first girl was some whore at CMA[111]. She was such a kink. She only wanted anal. ANAL... But yeah. Dude, I never got laid.

I didn't want to cheat on Katie. All those guys that fuck hookers, and cheat on their girlfriends – I hate them. I never wanted to do that. Katie knows it.

OK, so I'll tell you. But you gotta swear you won't repeat this to anyone. No one Ashore. You swear?

Alright. You know that story I told you about why I limp. Why my asshole always hurts? Well it wasn't

---

[111] CMA: California Maritime Academy. One of Seven Federally acknowledged and subsidized maritime academies.

because I nicked myself shaving. I made that up. My asshole is hurt man. Five fucking years I haven't been able to shit right. OK. So please don't tell anyone.

You know how I told you that I always have Katie take a strap on to me? Well we haven't done that in years dude. I want it so bad but my sphincter is ripped. Alright. Um... So, it was in Bangkok. I was on a three-month deployment as a third mate. The entire trip the only talk on the bridge was about fucking whores. Everyone. Fuck this. Fuck That. It's so cheap. It was gross. I was emailing Katie every night and jerking off like crazy. When we hit port, I went out with a bunch of the ABs[112]. We got fucking lit and they went out to this whore house and I just followed them. Dude. I let some little Asian bitch take a strap-on to me. She had me bent over and she couldn't get it in. I asked her to stop but she just rammed it in. My fucking asshole ripped dude. I seriously cried for an hour in that fucking whore house. I limped outside to a taxi and at 3 am I had to explain to the chief mate why I was going to a hospital and I lied. I said I had food poisoning. I went to a hotel and called Katie and cried and came clean with her.

She hung up on me and then wouldn't answer the phone. I bought plane tickets the next day and flew straight home and walked into an emergency room. I lied to the doctors for months and said that I took a

---

[112] AB: Able Bodied Seaman. An entry level position in the maritime, geared towards deck work.

really big shit, and that's why my ass was ripped. Katie wouldn't let me tell the truth. She said it didn't matter. But when I finally told a surgeon what had happened, he said that an impact tear is different than a pressure tear. To this day I have scar tissue from them sewing my sphincter back together. Jack, seriously, never put anything in your ass unless it goes in easy.

I feel horrible. I never wanted to cheat. We never have sex anymore. I haven't used a butt plug or been fucked in years.

YARN 76

GILMOUR, PO1

His email said he was reporting to Alameda in a month. The tone of the letter seemed like it was in boiler plate format, though I was excited none-the-less. It had been five years since I last saw Gilmour in San Diego. His new wife and him were driving out in a U-Haul and they would need help moving everything into their apartment. "It'll be a good time to drink beer and catch up!" *Gilmour!!!!*

In the years since the Thrill, we had only spoken sporadically and mostly by email. He'd aged and had become more private. Wise is a fair descriptor, but authentic was always my favorite. Gilmour had a hell of a career since we last parted and he was on the fast path towards Chief, and beyond. When he opened the moving truck's door, I was caught off guard by the expensive furniture... We spoke a few friendly words as we schlepped boxes and crates inside, but apparently it wasn't a good time to catch up, as he and his wife Amy needed to settle in. "We can catch up next week." I offered.

"Or the week after," he suggested. "Or whenever. I'll be pretty busy."

YARN 77

BRADLEY GREEN

Gilmour's return was anti-climactic. After leaving Bluejay in Maine, meeting the mother of my child(ren), and starting to work on ferries, I had mostly lost contact with my Coast Guard connections. Every so often I'd meet a veteran... I anticipated more debauchery and adventure with Gilmour, though he seemed to be over that phase of his life. That is, until he called me and gave me an offer. If I would be the designated driver for him and his group of Coasties, he would buy me a ticket to the Grateful Dead reunion show.

As a matter of principal, I hadn't cut any of my hair since leaving the Guard. It was to my nipples and my beard was to my belly button. Gilmour had landed a Government Vehicle for his outing and he passed the keys to me when he got to my place. Five other neatly trimmed guys were in the van, sitting in silence, pondering Gilmour's decision to let some hobo drive a GV.

Once we parked, I took off to find party favors in the lot[113], and soon found a handful of balloons. With a previously purchased 12 pack, tucked under my shirt, I skillfully walked by all the security to search for my straight edged friends. At the entrance to the stadium, a temporary fence corralled thousands of hippies through a security check point. To draw the attention of my crew (who had my ticket),

---

[113] "The lot," short for the parking lot at a Grateful Dead event (aka Shakedown Street). It is known as a safe place to find drugs, munchies and, if needed, to trip balls.

I jumped the fence and stood in the middle of the open area it created. "Gilmouuuuuuurrr!" Again, at the expense of my lungs, "Gilllmooooor!!!" It seemed useless, and I instantly became aware of the possibility of security barring me from entry. My mind piped the decision to inhale all of the balloons before I was caught. *Fuck it.*

Inhale

My attempt to sit failed and I fell to the ground in a moment of disheveled-bliss. There, I watched a balloon I had just untied, rush through the air like a mad bug. Other balloons started drifting upwards. A hand came into view. It snatched one of the balloon-strings from the air, and then that hand had a smiling face attached to it, and a second hand reached down towards me. "Hi. I'm Bradley," the smiling face said, and I was jerked to my feet. He then proceeded to untie the balloon he had rescued and huffed it down. *My last bit of nitrous.* "Gilmour is right over there. None of the other pussies would jump the fence so I had to come get you."

YARN 78

DONOVAN, PO3

onovan and I first met at my daughter's 2nd birthday. He arrived with his cousin, my good friend Gilmour. Obviously, a man of many interests, including music, Donovan became a face I would see often.

Hanging out at bars in Petaluma and café's around the Bay Area, Donovan would spend his off time, from his Coast Guard duties, playing blues and rock music on his electric-acoustic. To be blunt, behind a guitar he sounded like a fat black man out of the Mississippi Delta, or Adam Haworth Stephens singing "I Found a Love." I loved it. Take the stage away, and the guitar, and Donovan sank back into a normal straight-out-of-boot Coastie attitude. He was proud of making it through Coast Guard basic training, which made him hesitant to move forward in his music career – at the time he was attending a communications "A" school in Petaluma. Donovan was more-or-less quiet and distant in social scenes, until you asked him something slightly political or philosophical. And that's what I did often. We built our relationship over Donovan's armchair philosophies.

Through the course of a year, Donovan and I became closer and closer friends. He would come to my house and we would jam on the porch for hours as my daughter climbed around and tried to dance. He was also a drinker, and we would drive around the foggy coastal roads of Marin and Sonoma looking for dive bars and cafes to crash.

At some point Donovan was given orders to Hawaii. And he, like all shipmates do, weighed anchor and drifted away. And again I felt that subtle feeling of both loneliness and fear of missing the excitement. Hawaii! Just imagine.

Before Donovan left, Gilmour bought us tickets to a multi-day concert in the city, as a farewell offering. During this period of my life I had mostly no time away from my daughter. Any partying was done with her nearby. I hadn't really gone into a binge for months, and so that was my plan. In the field in front of the Bill Graham venue, I strolled looking for any and whatever drugs I could find. Zanex was on the menu that night and I scored four pills from some street kid. The night was amazing, and I danced my heart out, enjoying everything. Gilmour was enjoying the party with me, though Donovan was skeptical about trying a new drug, so he stayed sober.

The following morning my guilt was overwhelming and my energy exhausted. Gilmour and Donovan were still eager for me to go to the second night's show but I couldn't bring myself to do it. The mother of my daughter, Dev, decided to take my ticket and take a night off for her own peace of mind. I stayed home and focused on being a good dad. When I awoke the next morning, Dev wasn't home. With a baby who needed breast milk and a limited supply of frozen milk to give, I was pretty irate at Dev when she arrived the next afternoon completely hammered from the night before, like she had been tossed around by a tornado. She cried when she confessed to consuming a bunch of molly[114], and she wouldn't be breast feeding our kid for a few days. That disaster was not what our relationship needed at the time. I was too self-centered to manage any part of it, including my own emotions.

---

[114] Molly: another name for MDMA, Ecstasy.

And off Donovan went to Hawaii. Dev and I went on to have a second child. And Donovan went on to marry a beautiful Hawaiian girl named Jess. Life went on. And it did its thing. Dev and I started fighting heavily, and I left her, with the intent of spending only quality time with the kids and bettering myself, again.

JOURNAL ENTRY

(October 2010) Lois called me today. I haven't spoken to her since an awkward encounter on the banks of Lake Superior. She said that Stagger shot himself dead. She sobbed into the phone so I didn't catch everything said. Not that I cared too. She told me to check out the San Diego Papers. It took a few seconds to google it... Holy Fucking Shit!

YARN 79

BRADLEY GREEN

The nonskid felt the same. The water tight door was latched open, though I noticed its dogs were all attached to a quick acting lever. I could imagine Mr. B. giving a rambling lecture on Costa Rican culture. Deck-force siting stiff, cross legged. Kurtz leaning against fire-locker #1. Lee with dark shades, chewing on gum. Ray poking some new girl in the back. I could image Gilmour and Bluejay, half asleep, ready to hide in dry-stores... But now, it was Bradley doing the talking. With a small afro and a Nike shirt, he didn't look the part. He smiled at me – I wasn't moving, just zoning out. "Jack!"

I looked up and smiled. "Sorry. Just reminiscing."

"Come on man, let's smoke up here. Shut that hatch real quick so we can hear if anyone is coming."

I hadn't smoked weed on a boat since Alaska, ten years before. when paranoia cost me an entire evening. But Bradley had this endearing quality about him that made me relax and want to do what he was doing. As we moved forward of the boatswain hole the 1MC came on, "Now hear this. All family members please..."

Bradley started dogging the hatch mid announcement and I couldn't hear what was being asked of us. "Don't you want to hear that?"

"Nah. I don't give a shit. Do you?"

"I guess not." We moved forward one last door and we were standing above the hazmat locker. I told Bradley the story of huffing green-death in the paint locker. Memories were racing through my head. He started taking puffs and passed the joint my way.

Our children were on the mess-deck, playing pin-the-tail-on-the-pirate, or something similar. When Bradley invited me to come to the ship for his Wife's Open House, I wanted to say 'no,' but he said it would be a great time for the kids to hang out, and I was a bit curious to see what had changed since I left the guard. It was also fun to walk around a CG Cutter high, with a giant beard and a belly full of beer.

I was too high and began feeling paranoid. Bradley noticed right away. "Hey man. Haha. Don't worry about anything. You're good. Just follow my lead and we'll get the kids and head to the softball field to kick a ball around or something."

We strolled back through the 378 like we owned the place. We ran into Bradley's wife, Holly, and one of her shipmates on the second deck. They had just walked out of a berthing area. An awkward moment of uneasiness. I could tell Bradley was tense too, but we all smiled and we went up towards the mess-deck.

YARN 80
GIRTH, DECKHAND

H is name wasn't Girth, but he asked us all to call him Girth, so we did.

Girth wasn't the first sailor I'd met with major penis disproportionalism. A decade earlier I was at the MLEU, where I had a locker assigned between two guys with dongs roughly ten inches soft. Jacob on my left, and Rossi on my right. Jacob, on my left side, was a big old teddy bear guy, who said he couldn't have sex with his wife while she was pregnant; he had a dick that was easily the size of a ruler. On my right, Rossi, whose dick could wrap around his entire wrist and then some. Rossi was a fan of placing his member on bars, hanging out naked everywhere he wouldn't get arrested, and making fun of me in the locker room: "aw, look at that little guy. He must be shy." Rossi was a short funny Italian fucker.

A few years before meeting those horse-like-guys, I had a few run-ins with penises at boot camp. Our Company Colors[115] carrier used to walk around the shower room saying "gangway guidon," while he had an erect penis. I don't know how anyone could get a boner in the shower room at bootcamp.

There was a boot-camp erection exception. Morning-wood was common the week of our graduation. Just like every morning, we would be woken at reveille by our company commanders, whistles blowing, general shouting, shit being thrown across the room. We would jump out of our racks and line the center isle at attention. After a few moments the females of our company would arrive, walk

---

[115] Company Colors: each unit is provided with a flag (normally signal flags) which is symbolic of that unit and its mission/purpose. A guidon is the staff that the unit's flag is carried on.

swiftly down the center aisle, and arrange themselves in line at the far side of the barracks. The company commanders would then commence barraging us with orders, insults, and belittling comments. During the last week, everything was the same, except when we jumped out of our racks, the majority of us had morning wood – which is plausible due to the excitement of the coming graduation. When the ladies of the company walked by us, there were chants from both the women and us, "Gangway Guidons!"

But Girth was different. His dick wasn't that long. It was just thicker than a coke can. You could just look at the thing beside a can of cola and tell.

YARN 81

GILMOUR, PO1

Sandals, blue V-neck t-shirts and blue ODU[116] pants. The off-duty uniform of both Gilmour and Donovan. Donovan carried a guitar at all times. I wore a beard and sandals, short shorts, and old faded blue t-shirts. We sat around talking philosophy, politics, music. They had grown up around each other and had experience I could never imagine. But I saw Gilmour on The Thrill. Donovan's experience here, in San Francisco and Petaluma was nothing to what Gilmour and I experienced on that boat.

The drinks seem to hit me first, always, in any group. Boisterously I'd look for excitement and promote adventure. Donovan was slow to respond, though would get there with drink. Gilmour and Amy would leave, saying something about drinking and having to work the next day. Donovan and I would stumble to a park, lean back against some old Oak tree, and sing songs. Donovan, full of soul. Me, full of worry and regret.

Gilmour was the only shipmate I stayed in touch with who made it past a second tour, and into the path of retirement. He used to joke about people who would stay in, "lifers."

---

[116] ODU: Operational Dress Uniform

Worried about being conditioned. But none of us ever believe we are conditioned, and Gilmour doesn't think he is now. Maybe he's not. He's successful, no?

YARN 82

BLUEJAY

With a warrant out for his head in Panama, and all territories that ally with Panama, except the US, Bluejay's ability to travel for work were shot. Being excommunicated from maritime unions and losing his maritime credentials just sealed the deal. Back home he moved in on his brother's couch, and found a bar lawyer to fight his child custody case. Soon it was finalized. Bluejay lost all rights to see his children, was issued a restraining order against his wife and kids, and was levied a child support payment of half of what he made in the merchant marines. Bluejay went from Coastie extraordinaire to homeless, familyless, and drug addict in the course of a few years.

A manifested epidemic of deterioration hit Bluejay in waves, week after week. In a furry of opium induced angst, he jumped out of the third story window of his half-way house. Before pussying out and going feet first, instead of the other way, he called me and shouted his plans into my ear drum. I called the local police in Connecticut and they found him lying on the sidewalk, with a broken back, bruised spleen, smashed legs, and concussion. In his apartment they also found a plethora of drugs and paraphernalia. And unfortunately for Bluejay, he called his ex-wife like he had called me, which meant he violated his restraining order. After 3 months in a medical facility he was released to a psychiatric facility and awaited trial for various accounts of drug possession, assault, and violation of parole. After a year of further torment, suicide attempts, withdrawal and relapse Bluejay was sentenced to a five-year stent in state Prison. After three he was released on good behavior and he moved to the Bay Area, where our mutual friend Gilmour was just about to pack up his bags and move away.

Gilmour's farewell party was Bluejay's arrival party. We were sympathetic with Bluejay and extended all the help we could give him.

Knowing he was using, I couldn't spend too much time near him. Working at the Ferry Building in downtown San Francisco, I was able to catch up with him often on my way home from school or work. He'd talk about the fat girl he was fucking. The dyke bitch who sold him dope. The shows he couldn't afford to go to. His hair was inches longer each time I saw him, his face more somber. Big dark sunglasses and a cigarette. We'd lean against the railing, back to the Bay, and watch passersbys. Laugh about the old times. Mr. B. Gilmour. Clark. Lois...

I lost my job after I threatened to whack the vessel manager in his scrawny little chin. Bluejay lost his because he didn't show up. Unemployed, we'd sit at the Iron Horse saloon in Berkeley, getting reduced price beers from the bartender. Every now and then one of us would joke about sucking his dick as a tip, and one of us would consider it.

More jobs. Come and go. Relationship explosions. Loneliness. Struggle. Addictions. Melanoma skin accumulating, marks and folds. Hang out beneath the UC Berkeley Lighthouse (The Campanile), look up and the sky and clouds spin counterclockwise beyond the mighty 307' white stone structure. Stare at college girls, through dark glasses. Hold coffee mugs like they're railings. Chain smoke. Reminiscing like old men over a game of chess, just with no game of chess, and nothing to say. Our egos fade in and out, two wobbly steps forward, two steps back. Find a sea-stance. Weight-loss exposed bones. Coffee. Cigarettes. No ashtrays in Berkeley. No railing to flick the butts over – watch them float away in the wavy green grass.

Never speak of our children.

His cane is a carved piece of teak jetsam[117]. Red, in the shape of an anchor chain. He limps. Now, I pick him up at the marina. Meander like an old river, down the wooden docks when he's not in the parking lot. Each old rickety float leans, forces creaks, and wobbles. Gull shit and shells. Low tide. Bluejay walks with a straight leg. Hair to his lower back. Beard to his lower belly. Big dark shades. Always in long sleeves, even in hot weather. Cigarettes flying out the window as we drive around the back streets, browsing the corners.

---

[117] Jetsam: Objects jettisoned overboard, which have turned to debris and washed ashore.

YARN 83

DONOVAN, GM2

Missery Lounge had an open mic night I'd stumble to from my little studio basement apartment. Regular enough so they wouldn't throw me out, unless I was too drunk to talk right. They'd let me play Bob Dylan tunes. Pretend to be sober. Pretend to be Dylan. The bar owner was covered in tattoos, swallows and anchors, a whale across his lower back, props on his ass cheeks. His wife had the word "Ship" on her right butt cheek and he had the word "Mates" on his left butt cheek. If they mooned you at the same time, beside each other, it'd read "Shipmates," but I normally only saw "Ship."

During the day, I was doing contract work at marinas. Anything that had to do with fixing and mending boats. Diving, painting, rigging, and even piloting became my day-to-day. At some point I had scored a captain's gig with a wealthy guy out of Sausalito and he would throw huge cocaine parties, like we were in the 70's, on his 50' yacht as I would drive us around the Bay. I still knew a lot of the CG small boat members in that community, and I could often fend off boardings before they happened, just by radio chatter – and boardings were a lot more common in those days. On vessels there are no rules about drinking while driving, only driving while intoxicated, so I'd often antagonize the Coasties by holding up a bottle as they slowly cruised past. This made my supercargo[118] always laugh and he kept me on because I showed an edge of confidence

---

[118] Supercargo: the owner or stockholder of a vessel. A person of seniority above the captain, but not in charge of the vessel.

mixed with recklessness – both skillsets needed to maintain control on a vessel full of coked up wealthy white trash.

And this was my situation when Donovan moved back to the area.

Jess and Donovan were living in Coast Guard Housing, and I was in my Berkeley basement. Somehow, I managed to own a small sailboat during this time period of my life, and when Donovan contacted me, I demanded that him and his wife go sailing with me and the kids. Which is what we did. This instantly turned into a three-way friendship. Between Donovan, Jess and their dog, I was happy to have a social outlet in my life I could relate too. Donovan was stationed on a sister ship of the Thrill while he was in Hawaii and had traveled to many of the same port calls and seas that I had. We talked about the craziness of shipboard life, the swaying of the ship, and the disasters of Coast Guard politics and management styles. Donovan set up a "man cave" in his garage at Coast Guard housing and he used it as a place to get smashed and type away at an ancient typewriter he was obsessed with. A fan of Jack Kerouac, Donovan wanted to make every aspect of life an adventure – something we both had in common.

About a year after their move to the Bay Area, Jess and Donovan's relationship started fraying. Under Jess' desires, the relationship opened and Jess started seeing other men. Donovan explained to me that Jess had a lot of bad history (like family issues and marrying a homosexual Navy guy just to help him out). I watched Donovan go through a hell. A hell that seems all too typical of relationships in the maritime. You fall in love. You ravage and rave in the sack. You leave on a ship. You come back and find yourself alone, with a woman in your pocket, and stranger's dick on your mantel.

Donovan couldn't get Jess out of his head, and Jess needed Donovan's income to pay the bills. They were living separately. Donovan found escape in liquor and Jess found escape in friends. Donovan started gaining weight, and he was drenched in sweat each time I saw him. He'd pace the rooms and climb the walls, searching for some exit. I'd seen guys hurt and fall apart, though Donovan was different. His emotions were always turned in, like he was a sado-narcissist, devouring his body's attempt to produce serotonin by flogging it with vodka. He would ramble incoherently about his love for Jess and his need to have her back. Then he started talking about suicide. He couldn't deal with his head anymore. Then, he self-reported to the Coast Guard.

When you turn yourself in to the Coast Guard, and say things like "I am drinking too much," or, "I'm going to fucking kill myself," for whatever reason, the Coast Guard reacts in a preformatted way (policy before variables). The first step is preservation, then rehabilitation, then more preservation. During the rehabilitation portion of the ride, Donovan's suppressed memories surfaced and he was exposed to a torrential and violent storm.

Turns out Donovan joined the Coast Guard to get away from his grotesquely abusive Carolinian family. His escape led him to sea life: trapped between the melancholy ocean and hundreds of uniform seamen. His romantic visions of being a sailor failed him and he sought refuge with women, Jess. When Jess failed him, he sought refuge with alcohol. Then he relapsed to seek help from the Coast Guard. And the story may repeat itself.

Once again, I found myself wondering about the nature of Coasties. My Coast Guard days are over, yet here I am, amongst them. Long lost yarns resurfacing like a suppressed childhood horror. What type of people am I surrounding myself around? *Why do I surround myself with them?*

These bodies pile up like wrack on the beach.

YARN 84

BRADLEY, YN3

I n World War 2, the most dangerous job an American could have was in the Merchant Marines. The second most dangerous job was in the US Coast Guard. In 2003 the Coast Guard left the Department of Transportation and became the tip-of-the-spear for the Department of Homeland Security. We were both there for the change. Literally we changed from blue janitor uniforms to more stylish ODUs. The bow of each ship was stripped of its rescue-swimmer davit and a 50cal mount was installed in its place.

B radley was wearing a CG shirt which cleverly snuck in the words "coming to save the mother fucking day," into the CG shield. We sat on his couch pounding beers. One of Holly's shipmates, Jerry, was going through a divorce and was living with Bradley and Holly in their guest bedroom for months. In post 9/11 DHS Coast Guard, deployments were more frequent and lasted for longer periods of time. Holly and Jerry were drinking tequila in celebration of returning from one of these deployments. Bradley and I paid for a sitter to watch our kids all day and night.

The Women's World Cup was blasting on the big screen and we were all pretty well lit by half time. Other friends and neighbors wandered over and there was more drinking and eating. Jerry and Holly were in the kitchen a majority of the night and I could feel the tension radiating from Bradley. The game ended in a major upset when the US team lost in an overtime shoot out. Shots were brought out and the night drifted in. Bradley, Jerry and I were in the kitchen poking at chips and booze. Holly came out of nowhere wearing nothing but panties and a bra. Her long legs taunting us with purpose. Bradley yelled before I could process her entrance, "get some fucking clothes on woman!"

"You're not my fucking father, Bradley!"

"Babe! You can't just walk around like this."

"It's my fucking house, Bradley. I'll do what I want when I want." Her tone was of a raving drunk woman. She was flaunting her body to Jerry, in front of Bradley. *Oh shit.*

"I said get the fuck back in the bedroom!"

"Fuck you. Get your hands off me!"

Jerry jumped in, "Get your hands off her man!"

"Stay the fuck out of this Jerry. This is my wife."

Holly: "Fuck you Bradley, you're not my fucking boss."

I could find no solid footing, and my sealegs were useless in those types of situations. Bouncing back and forth, horribly uncomfortable. Jerry was wrong. Holly was wrong. Bradley was frantic. He wanted it all to stop. He responded too loudly, with aggression.

"Jerry. Let them figure it out dude. Let's get out of here."

We left the couple yelling at each other. I watched Jerry walk stiffly and with malice through the living room. He man-handled a half empty glass of beer with one hand as he chugged a gulp of tequila with the other. He stared at me with evil thoughts. Then he disappeared into his guest room. I walked out to my truck and lit a cigarette. Too drunk to see straight.

I was startled when the passenger door flew open. Bradley jumped in. "Let's go!"

"Where to my man?"

"Bar."

"Bar's closed."

"You got any booze at home?"

"Yup."

"Tequila?"

"Only."

YARN 85

JERRY, PO2

They knew each other for nearly a year. Jerry watched Bradley rejoin the guard, after being a stay-at-home-dad for two years. Jerry knew all of Bradley's secrets, all of them. He knew there was a fake rubber penis that excreted fake urine in Bradley's locker on base. When Jerry's affair with Holly became more than just about sex, he wrote an anonymous letter to Bradley's command.

> *"To CG Pacific Command,*
>
> *Petty Officer Bradley Green smokes marijuana daily. He has a fake urine device in his personal locker, in the gym on base.*
>
> *I prefer to keep myself anonymous, as I work with Petty Officer Green.*
>
> *Regards..."*

When Bradley was processed for discharge, his paper work read "Bad Conduct," for falsifying government documents.

Jerry fucked Bradley's wife each and every day, for 28 days, while Bradley was locked in rehab. He even made Bradley's kids cereal each morning. Later, Jerry moved Bradley's things out of his house and onto the curb. He then packed all his personal stuff into the room with Holly, in the drawers that used to be Bradley's. He even managed to get transfer orders to the same city as Holly a year later, New Orleans.

YARN 86

RAMBO

We used to strap our children to our backs and fish at a reservoir behind the Oakland hills. We both grew up fishing lakes, though reservoirs in California had more regulations than we were used to, so the catches were rare, but we weren't really there for that anyways. Before we became overwhelmed with parenting, Rambo would take us out on the San Francisco Bay on his homemade boat. He had built a 20' plywood and fiberglass boat in his garage over the course of a few months. If I didn't see him build it, I would have assumed he'd bought it off the shelf – he had skills and patience with projects like that. Out on the Bay we would fish for leopard sharks. Always launching in the mornings, before the sun was up, we'd take off with a cooler full of beer and gas station breakfast sandwiches. The wind starts howling near noon in the Bay Area, and we were always back at the loading ramp by then, drunken and tired. We'd catch shark, though we'd mostly reminisce about our younger days.

He left honorably, at the end of his four year tour. He joined for the GI Bill, and he left on schedule. Rambo is an example of the few who actually do this. A large percentage of veterans never use their GI Bill, others can't seem to graduate. Rambo, like me, did both, while starting a family.

As our friends slowly transferred out of the Bay Area, Rambo became more inclined to stay home, with his healthy and attractive wife. Other than a sporadic fishing trip, we only stayed in touch by texting grotesque photos back and forth. When he wasn't a tornado driver, he was a role model of balance and progress.

THE LAST SHIPMATE

"You get the fuck out of here and don't come back!... Pervert!"

I looked across the street in the direction of the shouting. I'd been searching the streets of Petaluma for a half an hour for Rambo. There he was. Stumbling. Tottering on the curb, leaning dangerously into oncoming traffic. Little control of his body, top heavy with a big wind – three sheets to it.

"Yo, Rambo! Run fucker. The truck's right here."

He saw me and darted into the road. A car went into a skid. Rambo slammed his fists onto the car's hood like Donkey Cong. He aggressively yelled something no one could understand, then bolted across the remaining portion of the street, dodging a second vehicle and horrified driver.

I yelled towards him, "this way dude!" And he ran towards me, jumped in my truck, and I hit the gas on to the main road. My left eye was closed to block out the double vision, and my right hand alternated between the gear shift and wheel, while my left hand held a cigarette out the window. The onramp to highway 101 had a slow mover on it so I used the emergency lane to speed around him.

"Fucking bad drivers man." Rambo was abnormally silent, and I turned up the radio. We didn't talk for the next five minutes.

"Hey, you really like this song huh?"

"Yeah, man. This is my shit."

And he turned it off, and looked out the passenger window without talking.

The Petaluma trip was the last time I saw him. A month later I called asking if he wanted to go fish the Delta. "Hey dude! Long time no see. Uh. No. I'm actually in Iowa right now.... Yeah we bought a house and everything... Hey man. Can I call you back? I gotta grab one of the kids real quick."

YARN 87

GILMOUR, CHIEF

Gilmour advanced to Chief recently. The CG sent him to Petaluma for pipelined training. This gave me the opportunity to hang out with the guy a little bit more, and the both of us looked much more defeated by life since we had last departed. The Thrill was 15 years early, and I had been separated from Dev by 5 years. Gilmour and I were in our mid 30's and life was moving fast. And though we both had love for sea and beer, our attitude towards responsibility and risks were different.

I brought up the Thrill in conversation and he soured. Said, he'd rather forget it. He called us "dumb kids."

"Ashore, I'm going to be a Chief now. I've done this stuff for 15 years and I'm over the games. This is my life. The Coast Guard's been good to me. It's been good to my family and the people I love. The fucking kids that join these days are worthless. No wonder Mr. B. was always an asshole."

I sat quietly.

YARN 88

CHARLES BLACK

He sits and stares. Face a mess of hair. Posts photo after photo after photo of orange and red sunsets on Instagram. Drinks malt liquor driving down the back-swamp roads, through the bayou. Says friendly things to strangers, sometimes comprehensible, sometimes a slurr of mumbled 'thank-ya-ma'ams'...

He now works for the Military Sealift Command. Two weeks on - two weeks off. When he's off, he lives in a trailer just above the confluence of the Missouri and Mississippi. From Charles's porch you can watch tugs with barge-trains move up and then move down the river. It's a good spot for Charles to sit, drink Reindeer Beer, and talk about his kid.

Charles's last duty station in the Coast Guard was in Port Angeles Washington. When Charles got kicked out of the guard for his first DUI, Charles and his pregnant girlfriend moved to a pot farm in an old logging field. When the child was born and his mother wouldn't stop using drugs, Charles got pissed and used a family loan to pay for a lawyer. In the eyes of Washington, Charles was the worse of the two parents (his Other Than Honorable discharge didn't help) and custody was mostly awarded to the mother. Charles was granted partial custody, and is allowed to have his son during the summer months. Eight years after that decree, Charles sits on his porch and laughs about the system that screwed him. When he is not underway with the MSC, Charles has a ritual in his home by the river. He chugs beer and crushes the cans into a ball with one hand, throws the garbage into a corner of his kitchen, and repeats the process until his sister-in-law cleans up the mess when he flies away for his next two weeks underway. On his boat he drinks in isolation and throws his trash overboard when no one is looking, then he posts photos of the sea on his Instagram account.

Back in the Coast Guard, Charles was the guy who wouldn't let anyone out drink him. He would drink while he was throwing up. In the MSC, he says he's protected by the unions and as long as he shows up, he won't get fired. "Shit," Charles says, "the operator gets fucked up with me on watch, haha."

YARN 89

GEORGIA, AMTC

Georgia was stationed in San Francisco. I only knew this because we were "friends" on Facebook. He never responded to my messages, until randomly he reached out to me, and asked if I would meet him in Sausalito for a drink. He apologized for the gap in communications. Curious, I had no reason not to go. Georgia used to be one of my best friends, and I always felt guilt for the way we left our friendship – me taking a cheap swing at him, because he had received orders to school before me. So, I found a sitter for the kids and headed for Sausalito.

Across the water Alcatraz Lighthouse was accentuated as the half way point between us and the city. Drinks in hand, we were sitting on a quaywall in Sausalito, exactly where "Sitting on the Dock of the Bay" was written 50 years earlier. San Francisco's lights were clear, and the lighthouse was abnormally bright each time it flashed. The container ship in the outbound lane was moving fast, and would soon be between us and the infamous island. Clanks and creaks from the wooden dock below as it lightly rocked against the piling. The night had gone as expected. Two old friends meeting in an awkward way, drinking beers, small and indifferent words.

"Ashore, you remember when I left the Thrill? You were pissed that I had orders before you?"

I looked at his face meaningfully for the first time in ages, knowingly he was saying something significant. It was dated, without joy.

"Man, I was the one that botched your paper work. When we signed up for school together, the BM1 told us that only one of us would get orders, but I knew you didn't hear. I finagled my orders to the top of the pile. I'm sorry."

Caught off guard, I looked down at the water below us. That had been so long ago. My night went from awkward, to comfortably jacked, to awkward again. Silence.

"That's not all... A few weeks after AMT school started, some shit went down. I've never told anyone, Ashore. My doctor thinks I should apologize to you, so I can move forward in my recovery. I've kept it hidden from everybody for years. It's the most fucked thing that could happen to somebody. Embarrassing. Painful. Fucking awful man. I never notified the command and no one on the Thrill knew."

I had no idea what he was talking about. I was about to tell him I didn't care. That I loved my last years in the Coast Guard and was thankful, if anything, of the way it turned out. But he started talking again.

"Do you remember a few years back? A Coast Guard Investigator questioned you about me?

I had forgotten about it. But it came rushing back to me. "Haha. I was drinking when they called. I remember clearly now, yeah. Something about a security clearance?"

"The questioning was really a gauge at my personality. They were trying to gather intel on me to know if they should take my word for the truth...." He sighed. "Ashore. I was raped by a group of Navy guys in Norfolk."

More silence.

"My class flew to the Naval Air Station there to train on Carriers. A group of guys jumped on me in the barracks. I was drinking, as normal, and a bunch of guys invited me to their dorm. When I got there one of them just pounced on me. They fucking raped me."

He stopped talking. His head was bent down. We sat still. I couldn't say anything other than "Fuck, dude, I'm sorry." The dock below kept rocking. The lighthouse flashed. The city was now submersed in a fog. The passing ship, gone.

YARN 90

BRADLEY GREEN

On the streets, out of the Guard. No more boats. For five years, Bradley struggled to make sense of it all. He started couching surfing. Watched his wife and her lover transfer and move into an apartment together. He followed to be near his kids. Bottles of liquor every day, starting early. Drunken calls:

> *"Hey.. ug. I'm a desperate despairing drunkard...*
> *Dancing in the hall. Hands over head.*
> *Diamond shaped, like a pig ballerina.*
> *Who are we? Bradley?*
> *Gilmour?*
> *Donovan?*
> *Spinning. Spinning. Spinning.*
> *We dreamed of sober seas.*
> *Never afraid of living.*
> *Your love left, Ashore. My love left.*
> *Suffer. Pathetic on the docks below.*
> *Bubbling beer stains your upper lip, amber.*
> *It's aerated your brain.*
> *Who are you? Bradley?*
>
> *Did she fuck him? Did he fuck her?*
> *Does it make you think?*
> *We run the trail. Sleep the night cold.*
> *Whiskey doesn't freeze. Dehydrated despair.*

What did they do on deployment?
Fuck in the line locker? Quick to cum.
Juices everywhere?
She was my wife! I can see her face.
What did she want from the sea?
That was my escape."

He met guys who were making it big in the California Pot Industry, and success followed. Excitement and money. Orgies with big cowboy dicked southerners. Access to his kids and wife waned. He was driving through Texas, at the night time speed. Traffic stop on the freeway and there were drug dogs. Sniffing all the cars. Arrested for drug trafficking. 100lbs of marijuana stuffed in a duffle bag which had a Coast Guard patch, shield and anchors, sewn just above an old faded black stencil that read "SA B. GREEN

I speak with Bradley a few times a year through slow mail. He received a 15-year sentence from a voting population who wears synthetic clothing and plastic cowboy hats. *Spun, no doubt, on plastic yarns.*

Four years in the US Coast Guard, submersed in dirty sailor company every step of the way... *Maybe your prison room suite will be on an island, a view of faithful gulls flying through the glass-sea-like skies.*

YARN 91

GEORGIA, GONE

Sitting on a boat/swaying side to side
smelling the life/of morning lowtide
First he floats/Then he sinks
On the rail/I sit and thinks

We tried to rekindle our friendship while he lived in the city. We went to a few Grateful Dead cover shows together. Stumbling around like we had aged twenty years since the San Diego adventures. And as time went on, our friendship grew. Always slightly despondent, Georgia never said much more about what was on his mind other than comments about music.

> *Journal Entry: (June 2012) My first concert was with Georgia, at the Forum in Los Angeles, The Red Hot Chili Peppers. I think I picked up Anthony Kiedis' autobiography because he is back in town. Kiedis is a mad man. Reminds me of Bradley's energy level. Paranoid on Pot. Addicted to everything. Go. Go. Go....*

> *Georgia brought up the New Year's Dead show in Oakland, 2003/04. I didn't think he remembered it like me. Dancing. Clowns. Ballerinas. Midgets. A*

double dose of Mushroooms. First 1/8th didn't work. Second 1/8th kicked in as we started feeling the first one. Running up the handicap ramp. Spinning with fat girl. Georgia on the floor. I see my hand reach for his chest. He doesn't move. Panic. Stand up. Head down. Walk away. I hear people say, 'oh my god he's just leaving his friend there.' I sit and put my head in my lap. Georgia walked over. 'Hey fucker! We gotta get out of here!' Hey was alive! More midgets on the train. Dodging burning traffic cones on the freeway. Georgia shaking his head. 'You left me for dead fucker.'

In the course of a year our friendship had grown again. He called me out to a bar one night, and when I said I had the kids he asked in a serious way if I could get a baby sitter.

He said he had developed colon cancer, which was most likely the result of HPV, perhaps from being fucked by the Navy. He reached out to me after his doctors had given him a poor survival percentage.

The tumor in his colon was successfully removed, though the blood test six months afterwards were bad. The cancer was back and spreading rapidly. Georgia sent me a sealed envelope with directions to open it in the event his mother contacted me. He was put on a harsh regiment of chemo-therapy, weakened, and died at the age of 35.

've sat so many times under the Golden Gate Bridge, in pea-soup fog, listening to the sound of the horn in the fog, smelling lowtide, rocking with the hair-of-the-dog. Never thought I'd have to do it while my friend's nephew dumped ashes into the outgoing tide, just like Jerry Garcia. I had snuck a cd player on board and turned the volume up on "He's Gone," as the ashes drifted away, as his letter asked. Each and every face on board took the music in stride, and with a smile.

"Rat in a drain ditch. Dogs in a pile.
Nothing left to do but smile, smile, smile."
(Dead)

YARN 92
STAGGER LEE, CG VET

I liked Stagger. I still do. I like the idea of him. On a boat for years and he never saw the water. When I left the Thrill, I never looked back and I never spoke the name Stagger again, until Lois called me.

I read the article after I hung up on Lois. Memories flooded my brain. Stagger in shades, leaning in the boatswain hole. Stagger in latex gloves, on hands and knees, cleaning. Stagger brushing his teeth. Stagger cooking rice, Sriracha sauce at the ready. Stagger in a dark parking lot. Leans in my window and smiles really big. Stagger with a sidearm, pressed uniform, straight face, hard jaw, clenched smirk. Mr. B.'s ceremonious dance, honoring the long-term deckie for his style and swagger. Swagger Stagger Lee.

THE SAN DIEGO YELLOW PRESS

While defending his drug network and adobe, Stagger Lee barricaded himself in his home with his girlfriend. The police became fed up with his antics and crashed down his front door. Stagger ran for his bedroom with his girlfriend, chased by a K9 named Danté. He stabbed the pursuing dog more than twenty times. The first cop burst through the door, which was not dogged properly, and Stagger shot him center mass. The officer fell, his partners retreated. Lying on the floor, the officer raised his gun again and looked up to see Stagger and his girlfriend panting. "Adios bandido," was the cleverest thing Stagger thought to say before shooting the cop again, this time in the head. His girlfriend was screaming. "AAAAAGGGGHHHHH!!!! AGGGHHHH!" Distraught from years of social dissonance and methamphetamine abuse, Stagger couldn't concentrate and he shot her too. "I can't fucking think, Ho!" He grabbed his phone. No answer. Leave a message – "Bye Kurtz, the cops are here," click. Stagger looked down at his finger outside of the trigger guard. Yelled through the door at the police on the other side. "FUCK YOU MOTHER FUCKERS!!!!!!!!!!!!!!!!! FUCCCCCKKKKKKK. ARGGGGHHHHHHHH"

BANG!

YARN 93

DONOVAN, GM2

I was working aboard Alcatraz Passenger Ferries for the National Parks Service. My inexperienced Captain was a decade younger than me, but he had a dick twice the size of mine. I had befriended a deckhand, a salty kid named Dan, and had encouraged him to get his merchant mariner credential. When Dan said he needed to drive to San Diego for the weekend, and Donovan contacted me saying he was leaving rehab and had a week of free time to kill, we all teamed up and rode with Dan down Highway 5 to San Diego.

In San Diego, Donovan announced he would rent a room for himself, and that we "shouldn't bother him until it was time to go," as he needed to free his mind and type. Every so often we'd catch a glimpse of Donovan opening the door for a lady-boy or cracked-out prostitute.

The morning of our last day, Dan went to his class, and I went to get Donovan, anticipating the need to pull him together and toss him in the shower. He wouldn't answer his door and I finally convinced the front office manager to let me in the room. When the door opened, a thick fog of cigarette smoke came barreling out. Seeing the concern of the hotel manager, I quickly jumped in the room and slammed the door shut behind me. There was a bathroom light on and through the burning smoke I could make out a figure on the bed. I found the main light and soon saw Donovan sprawled out over his bed, ass naked. He was bloated and caked in sweat. There was a full ashtray on the bed beside him, with a cigarette still burning. *Good he's not dead.* His type writer sat on the bed side desk and torn paper was everywhere. Bottles of liquor scattered; ten, twenty maybe, all empty.

"Donovan? Donovan? You alive bud?"

A few mumbles and a throat clear. He remained face down as he talked. "Ashore, you remember when I went to that show with Gilmour and Dev?"

"Yeah, why bud?"

"I fucked Dev that night."

POJACK ASHORE, STUDENT

Old man down, down by the docks of the city, couldn't see me. He asked me for a cup of coffee.

"Well, I got no money. You can drink mine, fella, if ya tell me a story."

"My name is August West..." (Dead, p. Wharf Rat)

Bluejay wasn't aware of my reasons for meeting under the Campanile. Almost by coincident, it was the perfect location between our two homes. And my classes were nearby...

THE CAMPANILE

When Richard Henry Dana Jr. returned to San Francisco in 1859 he was struck silent by the tremendous change. Ten years earlier the entire state of California was obtained by the United States, which seemed arbitrary, as the fur industry was drying up with the near extinction of the furry animals there. As if some sort of conspiracy was at play, gold was discovered in the eastern portion of the State months after the USA acquired it. San Francisco Bay was the mouth that fed the gold rush – then it was the asshole that shit it out. The number of sailors entering the bay grew by the tens of thousands, year after year, in that short decade. Interested in the first true economic "gold mine" of its existence, the United States sent the Army to supervise the chaos. The Army erected its first fort on Alcatraz Island, along with a lighthouse in 1855, to warn every sailor who passed through the Golden Gate Straits of who was in charge.

The vessels entering the Bay were all ocean-going boats, which were forced to land in the deep waters against the San Francisco City front. Within years, derelict boats were the primary threat to undermining the gold industry[119]. The Army responded by building a citadel on Alcatraz with prison and gallows. Sailors and Captains caught abandoning their vessels would be charged, confined and even hung on Alcatraz Island (imagine the six-month voyage to San Francisco, with little to do other than spin yarns over the newly discovered Gold! You'd abandon your ship too). As Dana passed through the Golden Gate, he saw Alcatraz Lighthouse, and he was perturbed by it – he knew it wasn't a beacon, it was an intimidator.

---

[119] Undermine: to dig beneath the foundation; create instability. It's ironic to undermine a mining operation. And it's absurd, but true, that seafarers threaten the stability of gold mines – assuming you frame with economy in mind. Maybe the gold threatened the stability of seafarers!

On Dana's return visit he met with California's governor Henry Haight. The two spoke about the dire need to help the growing society of misfits, adventure seekers, and law breakers. As a lawyer, Dana was mainly interested in establishing a school of law. As a public officer, Haight was interested in a little more. The rough outlines were introduced to erect a school for failed miners and sailors, using federal money set aside for new land-owners to develop their land for agricultural purposes. And as a little icing on the cake, Dana requested a lighthouse structure to be built to overpower the medieval light on Alcatraz. It took less than five years for California to purchase and begin building (1865) what is now the UC Berkeley campus, on the eastern side of San Francisco Bay. The campus' lighthouse did not receive its funding but was noted in the initial planning stages.

At the turn of the 20th century, a successful writer sat down at Heinold's Saloon with the head of UC Berkeley to discuss the social problems evolving from the school. Upset by the high-class population overwhelming the school, and destroying its original mission to provide for the low class, Benjamin Wheeler asked Jack London to be a guest lecturer for a semester, to help draw in a more diverse population of students. This conversation made little progress, as Jack London was anxiously awaiting the opportunity to set sail across the Pacific. However, Wheeler told the "Dana-Lighthouse" story to London. Jack made a few calculations and noted that a lighthouse built in the correct location on the campus, would act as a giant range marker when accounting for the center of the Golden Gate Strait and the Alcatraz Lighthouse. Jack was tickled by this and volunteered his time to progressing the concept.

By 1905 London found a private contractor to build the structure and, pending his return from a planned voyage around the globe, he committed to drumming up interest in the campus, via the iconic lighthouse and all that it represented. Then a major event happened: in 1906 a major earthquake sent the plans of building a tower into oblivion and Jack London's sailing vessel was battered by a small tsunami that swept through present day Jack London Square (this tsunami was caused by a chunk of Yerba Buena Island falling into the Bay, which sent a wall of water 5 feet high rushing through the Oakland Estuary). The following year Jack was occupied repairing his vessel and setting sail for Hawaii.

In 1908 the Alcatraz Lighthouse was demolished, due to the earthquake's damage from two years before. A taller lighthouse was built on the opposite side of the island within a year.

In 1909, a prominent Berkeley resident dropped dead, and his wife agreed to donate the family fortune to UC Berkeley, if they agreed to erect a monument to honor her husband. The campus agreed and the plans for the Lighthouse were thrown into the spotlight once more. The widow, last name of Sather, didn't like the concept of a light beacon, and agreed to the plans only if the light was replaced with bells instead. No person was present to argue on behalf of the original plans, and the tower was donned with bells instead of light. Also, no one understood Jack London's plan to align the tower with the Lighthouse on Alcatraz, and when the Alcatraz Lighthouse was rebuilt in a different location to the south, the Campanile's location became off centered – ruining a perfect range marker for the campus and the Golden Gate Straits by a significant 2 degrees North.

Jack London returned haggard from sea-sickness and tropical infections. Upon his return he noted the Campanile in the distance, off centered, with no light, and his spirits failed him. He refused to promote the Sather Tower, the Campanile, or the University. And the working sailor once more was placed at a disadvantage, due to some wealthy bitch and her affection for bells.

Unfortunately, schools around the states are still attended by the privileged, instead of the needy; and sailors have some of the lowest attendance and graduation rates. But a good idea is a good idea, and an industrious student from UC Berkeley learned of his campus' start and the tragedy of the Campanile. For the tower's 100th year (2013) he designed a giant "solar beacon" which could attract attention from ships entering the Golden Gate, finally! (Vallerga, 2013)

Bluejay and I sit smoking by a "no smoking" sign, beneath the 300 foot tower. He's ignorant of the tower's history and the reason I choose to come here. He stares at young women through his shades, as I gaze in wait for incoming ships. Maybe it will be me on lookout...

Flick cigarettes into the wavy grass. Don dark sunglasses... Sailors should never become wrack.

Shit. I'm going to be late for class.

LINE

• • •

Decision Review Officer,

As I was saying, how's this for "INSUFFICIENT?" Assholes. And now that I have it out, I have doubt. Hahaha. Maybe if I added a few explosions, or falls from the jack-cross, you'd find this more compelling? Maybe these yarns will be made into my noose. Or maybe, without any luck, it will be braided into a Captain's Daughter, and come to rest on my gingerbread work[120].

I digress...

I wonder which Ad won me over as a righteous kid. Which image? Are there any studies on false advertising and customer unhappiness? We bought into values that never existed as such. Everyday heroes. Dignity and Pride. Nationalism. The Coast Guard's message: Honor, Respect, Devotion to Duty: "Perception is everything."

Looking back. My post was to protect an image. "Officer Presence, and the rest follows," is what they said. I'm sure that façade has done wonders for the people labeled "Other Than Honorable." It's worked

---

[120] Gingerbread Work: the detailed and skilled wood carvings on the stern of a 15th or 16th century carrack or galleon. Shitting off the stern of a vessel is prohibited because it will ruin the gingerbread work.

its magic on the head of those on barstools, on helm-stools, and standing on the quay waving.

Where is the win-win with that perception philosophy? Authenticity is what we need. Real humans on both sides of the bulwark.   I'll listen to a man who tells the truth despite its short-term costs, faster than a man with a fake smile and hand-shake. Those plastic faces are the first symptoms of betrayal. The Art of Perception doesn't hold up universally in the age of information - the lies are now preconceived because of The Art's long-term use.

Who is fighting for the beacons? Who fights for the intimidators? Who's standing guard over all this suffering? This senseless drama.

My lungs are sore. My throat is more coarse. Bradley's drooling over there on the typewriter. He's 'bout drunk I suspect. Time to put this thing on the hard[121].

You know which dock I sail from,

Pojack Ashore

---

[121] On The Hard: a literal reference to hauling a ship onto land, for repairs.

SHIPMATES

Works Cited

Affairs, D. o. (2018). *VA National Suicide Data Report 2005–2016.* USA: USA.

Dana, R. H. (1840). *Two Years Before the Mast.* Boston: Houghton Mifflin Co.

ICF International, I. (2013). *State of Behavioral Health of the United States Coast Guard.* USA: USCG's Health, Safety & Work-Life Directorate .

London, J. (1999). *The Sea-Wolf.* USA: Dover Publications, Incorporated.

Maesfield, J. (1902). *Bill.* Salt Water Ballads.

Melville, H. (1986). *Billy Budd and Other Stories.* USA: Penguin Publishing Group.

Mills, L. F. (2019). *Abandoned Shipmate: The Destruction of Coast Guard Captain Ernie Blanchard.* North Carolina: McFarland.

Steinmetz, S. I. (2011). *The Study of a Secret Society: Resistance to Open Discussion of Suicide in the United States Coast Guard.* Dissertation.Com.

SHIPMATES

ABOUT THE AUTHOR

Bradley Angle served his enlistment in the US Coast Guard from 2002 to 2007. His service started on a sea going Cutter, which traveled from the Equator to the coast of Russia. His latter career was in Maritime Law Enforcement, where he spent countless deployments throughout the coastal states. Bradley left the Coast Guard honorably, as an E-4, as a result of his second Mast.

From 2009 to the present, Bradley has worked on multiple entrepreneurial projects and he actively operates a source for scanty maritime information under the name Dirty Sailor Company (www.dirtysailorcompany.com). With a degree in Behavioral Science and a Master's in Business Admin, Angle focuses on his life's passions: the maritime socio-cultural environment. His ultimate goal is to understand the relationship between maritime culture and shoreside communities, and how that relationship adapts to shifts in technological, environmental, economic, social and regulatory conditions.

BRADLEY UNCENSORED

In South Hawaii, I sat in olivine sands, allowing the uprushing swash to force grit and salt over my naked lap. Gazing at the water, I disappeared into a dimension of polychromes and dreams. There I basked in some sort of great feeling of wonder, which I've never been able to articulate to others. This same polychrome feeling existed twenty years ago, when I signed my enlistment papers for the United States Coast Guard. They surely tried to scrub it off.

- BTA

Made in the USA
Las Vegas, NV
14 February 2023

67537590R00194